IT'S ALWAYS BEEN OURS

IT'S ALWAYS BEEN OURS

Rewriting the Story of
Black Women's Bodies

JESSICA WILSON

NEW YORK

Hachette Go, an imprint of Hachette Books
Hachette Book Group
1290 Avenue of the Americas
New York, NY 10104
HachetteGo.com
Facebook.com/HachetteGo
Instagram.com/HachetteGo

First Edition: February 2023

Hachette Books is a division of Hachette Book Group, Inc.

The Hachette Go and Hachette Books name and logos are trademarks of Hachette Book Group, Inc.

The publisher is not responsible for websites (or their content) that are not owned by the publisher.

Print book interior design by Linda Mark.

Library of Congress Cataloging-in-Publication Data has been applied for.
ISBNs: 978-0-306-82769-3 (hardcover); 978-0-306-82771-6 (ebook)

Library of Congress Control Number: 2022946640

Printed in the United States of America

LSC-C

Printing 1, 2022

Introduction

Breathe Beauty

M Y WAITING ROOM AND OFFICE SPACE COMMUNICATE EVERY-
thing I want patients to know: that my work centers those too
often overlooked by my fellow dietitians—Black women, femmes,
and queer folks. The bookshelves display covers that address body
politics and queerness; the walls are hung with artist Alillia's life-
size paintings of Black bodies, unapologetic in their abundance. My
favorite, *Breathe Beauty*, greets me in the waiting room every time I
walk out of my office. The figure in the painting has dark skin with
gold highlights around nose and eyes. The figure is naked from the
shoulders up, face framed by blue-black, kinky hair falling around
the shoulders. Dark, full lips form part of the violet butterfly that

1

is painted around the mouth. The figure's strong gaze strikes me as empathetic and calm, a welcome presence in an office that holds many emotions.

Mia is in the waiting room, perched on the edge of my couch wearing a pressed navy pencil skirt and a pink silk blouse with pearl buttons. I glance up at *Breathe Beauty* as I exit my office and greet her. Knee bouncing, Mia's black spiral-bound notebook is moving up and down on her lap. She has relaxed hair that reaches past her shoulders. It is nine a.m. on a Saturday and, though many of my clients would arrive in casual attire, Mia is dressed to be taken seriously. I am curious about whether she has not been heard or respected by previous clinicians.

As we walk into my office, I turn on the noisemaker for privacy and invite her to have a seat on my black leather loveseat. It's overcast in Oakland that morning; she looks out the window as she gets settled.

We exchange pleasantries before I let her know what she can expect from me: honesty, curiosity, and a political context for her experiences. I find that sharing my style up front reduces anxiety for my clients and allows me to connect with them more quickly. One hour is very little time to hear a Black woman's body story.

Within minutes Mia's story unfolds. She's here because she's exhausted, so exhausted that even a good night's sleep does not restore her. She's recently changed medical insurance and met with a new doctor who told her that her lab results show signs of malnutrition, which is how she ended up in my office. Also, at her last salon visit she and her hairdresser realized that her hair is thinning and also has stopped growing. The hairdresser recommended some supplements for hair growth, and Mia is hoping to get my feedback on these, as well as supplements that can fix her deficiencies and increase her energy.

Mia is twenty-four and has just started graduate school in a town close to home. She is in a predominately white aerospace engineering program, the only Black woman in her class. Six months prior to starting her program she embarked on a "Wellness journey" after her previous doctor told her that she was "obese." That doctor told Mia she needed to lose weight to reduce her risk of developing chronic diseases, ones that she is more likely to get anyhow because she is Black. At twenty-four, apparently Mia needed to be concerned about the ways she is likely to die as a Black woman. Her body, from that appointment on, was a risk factor. Mia hadn't thought of her body in such a pathologizing way prior to that appointment. Hearing how the doctor problematized her body was disturbing to Mia; she lost the weight he recommended and more. She scoured the internet for advice and looked up ideas for "healthy meal prep." She stopped eating meals with her family and instead brings over her own containers of food to eat while they share food her mom has prepared. She started going to the gym every day and is now worried to take a day off.

The response to her weight loss has been overwhelmingly positive. She has noticed a shift in her social capital and desirability. Her peers and professors have started looking at and talking to her differently. Her classmates know how much she exercises and praise her for taking the time to do so when the academic workload is so overwhelming they don't even have time to sleep. Mia appreciates the feedback and interprets this to mean that she is disciplined and Healthy in their eyes. But Mia doesn't engage with her peers outside of classes because she needs to exercise. She also doesn't join them for happy hour because she doesn't want to pay for a side salad—the only thing she eats at restaurants—because she could make the same thing at home for less money. And besides, the alcohol is just extra calories that she doesn't need.

I ask Mia about her days, and ask more specific questions about how much she is eating and how much she is exercising. I ask her which supplements she is already taking. We discuss what messaging she got about food and bodies as she was growing up. As we continue to talk, she gets visibly impatient. She tells me that she came here for me to tell her what is missing in her diet so that she can take supplements to make up for it, that's all. I realize that my attempts to build rapport aren't what's needed in this moment and decide to be clear about my concerns. I tell Mia that her energy levels will likely improve and her hair may grow back if she begins to eat more food and exercise less.

I see the confusion on her face, the subtle frown line and slightly raised eyebrow. She tells me, "That can't be the problem; what I've been doing is *working*, it's getting *results*. There's just a vitamin or mineral missing from my diet; maybe magnesium?"

"I understand your concerns," I share, "but from what you've told me I don't have concerns about your vitamins and minerals, I have concerns about calories, fat, and protein."

"But I'm the healthiest I've even been in my life! I eat intuitively now, my body doesn't like any of the foods that I used to eat; it prefers vegetables and fruit."

Her body is no longer a risk factor.

When I ask Mia if anyone has expressed concerns about her food restriction and rigidity, she assures me this isn't what's going on here—it's not about weight loss or the thin ideal; it's about her health and feeling good in her body. I ask whether people have talked subtly about her food, and she tells me that her sister has noticed what is going on and offered to support her. But Mia doesn't need support; she just needs me to tell her how to fix the problem so that she can get her energy back and thicken her hair.

I hear this regularly. It's not about dieting. It's about "Health" and "Wellness." It's about feeling "clean." And because this pursuit of Wellness also feels like a pursuit of purity and morality, she is happy to perform whatever rituals or sacrifices may seem necessary to contain her body.

I explain to her how energy deficits impact the body and why this would explain her experiences and lab results. She listens, opens her mouth to say something, and then pauses. She looks out the window and becomes tearful. "I can't be the only Black person in my class and also be fat," she says. And there it is, the reason why Mia is here: the impacts of white supremacy on the body narratives of Black women and the safety found in conforming to what whiteness demands.

All I can do is nod.

Black women are tasked with existing in a society that views us as disposable.

The politics and constructs that shape society shape our bodies. White supremacist capitalism objectifies and commodifies individuals. It creates social hierarchies and then makes money by selling us the promises of thinness, Health, and, ultimately, whiteness.

Mia and I discuss the impacts of white supremacy on the desirability of Black women. I let her know, without judgment, that I understand how conforming to what whiteness demands makes us more palatable in predominantly white settings. We discuss how straightening our hair, restraining ourselves, taking up less space—both figuratively and literally—and even lightening our skin can make it easier to get a job, a partner, and a home loan. We discuss how we have survived living in a world that doesn't value Black women by negotiating physical and psychological stress and trauma daily.

I tell Mia that I often see marginalized people engage in practices that can negatively impact their well-being in order to lessen microaggressions, organize their day-to-day actions, and strategize existence. Navigating a competitive, predominantly white graduate program is hard enough. Mia tells me she fears that if her body conforms to the stereotypes of Blackness that her classmates have, she may finish the program but won't have the networks she'll need to advance in her career. In Mia's mind, becoming thin is not about being a certain dress size; it is about survival. If others perceive her body to be a disciplined body, she knows she will be treated with more respect by classmates and professors.

I share that I know she began her Wellness journey with the best of intentions. And that I understand how the positive feedback and attention she's getting for having lost weight make it easier to navigate everyday life.

Mia is quiet. I am quiet, too. I want her to take her time. After a minute or two, her feelings bubble up.

She wipes a tear from her cheek and tells me that, though she may agree with me in theory and understands that eating food may give her more energy, she just can't gain weight—it's too much of a risk. In fact, she would like to lose more weight "to be safe."

I know.

Our safety is contingent on how little of a threat we pose to those around us. If we can make ourselves smaller both literally and figuratively, we may be able to uncouple ourselves from the savagery associated with our Blackness.

Our humanity is tied to how well we can conform to what whiteness demands. We might swallow parts of ourselves, rather than food, to become more palatable to others. We may hold ourselves and other Black women to higher standards than we would any other group of people. We seek respect, and get tripped up in respectability.

Our survival in society directly correlates with our resilience. We push ourselves beyond capacity to get through our day-to-day tasks.

• • •

THIS BOOK IS ABOUT BODIES AND HOW BLACK WOMEN ARE TOLD to have them.

The dominant narratives about all bodies were crafted centuries ago and continue to be told today. From birth, our body sets expectations for those around us. This book makes the case for rewriting those narratives, for putting Black women at the center of the narratives, rather than having our stories filtered through a white lens. I use the body as a vehicle with which we can conceptualize how these stories have shaped our lives and how we might rewrite them going forward.

I use the body as the vehicle for storytelling because, as Isabel Wilkerson puts it in her book *Caste: The Origins of Our Discontents*, it is a flashcard by which we are viewed and judged in our society. It signals race, gender presentation, visible ability, age, size and shape, and class. Wilkerson notes of the race-based caste system in the United States: It's "an artificial construction, a fixed and embedded ranking of human value that sets the presumed supremacy of one group against the presumed inferiority of other groups."[1] She provides a global view of the ways in which caste has shaped this country and a complex argument for the ways in which Blackness and whiteness have been artificially constructed. She argues our bodies signal "traits that would be neutral in the abstract but are ascribed life-and-death meaning in a hierarchy favoring the dominant caste whose forebears designed it."

Noting the fluidity of race and the shifting requirements for those assigned whiteness, Wilkerson says, "Race is what we can see, the physical traits that have been given arbitrary meaning and become shorthand for who a person is. Caste is the powerful infrastructure that holds each group in its place."

The caste system exists because of the racial distinctions between bodies, and I argue it lives on in our bodies. It relies on the meaning and narratives we assign to bodies. This meaning impacts the ways in which society celebrates, tends, penalizes, and pathologizes people in the United States and other Western and colonized countries. Our bodies are pivotal in the assignment of power and privilege.

I use *caste* rather than *race* when referencing the impacts of white supremacy. Caste is governing, while racism is often attributed to personal bias. Books, TED Talks, articles, and corporate diversity, equity, and inclusion (DEI) presentations provide audiences with the simple one-to-one solutions to bias. Racism is positioned as both a conditioning and a failing of the individual. The complexities of race are simplified to how we feel and what we think about one another. We're told that we're relying on stereotypes and "making assumptions" when perpetuating anti-Blackness. Race is regularly pitched as an interpersonal concern rather than a structural one, which makes the case that we can unlearn race. Even if individuals unlearn the set of rules assigned to skin color, unless something changes, we will still all be bound by the systems of caste in society.

• • •

I COME TO THIS BOOK WITH BOTH MARGINALIZED IDENTITIES AND privilege. I am a queer, Black woman, with an uncontrolled seizure disorder, all of which impact my experience and interactions in this world. I am also mixed race, with looser-textured hair, which makes me more palatable as a Black woman. I have an advanced degree, and my profession offers me a livable wage. I am thin. Though I will speak about a variety of lived experiences, I am only an expert of my own and bound to make mistakes when speaking about the experiences of others.

This book talks a lot about fatness as well as Blackness. Even though I experience "the residue of anti-fatness," as Bryan Guffey puts it in an episode of the podcast *Unsolicited: Fatties Talk Back*, I do not experience the violence directly, and as such, readers will benefit from seeking out the writings of others and learning directly from their experiences as well.

You'll see a lot of me in this book. Much of its content has come from my experiences as a dietitian who remains both hypervisible and erased in my profession. I am one of the 3 percent of Black dietitians who make up the field. In my coursework I was "taught" about Black people and what "they" eat and what to tell "them" about nutrition. Similar to Mia, I was taught that the bodies of Black people are inherent risk factors just for existing. In my training decades ago and at conferences into the 2020s, I have heard about Black people's individual responsibility to take three buses to get to a grocery store to buy whole grains and leafy greens: quinoa and kale. Southern food is constantly vilified by dietitians and directly associated with Black people at the same time hipsters and gentrifiers are enjoying a renaissance of ribs, pork belly, greens, okra, mac and cheese, chicken and waffles, and cornbread. When the same foods that are pathologized in the context of Blackness are associated with thin, white, affluent people, they become a foodie's gastronomical paradise. Bay Area residents can enjoy a lemon-lime Alameda Point craft soda with their BBQ pork riblets from Jupiter, a brewhouse in Berkeley, all while shaming and taxing those who buy Sprite from the corner store.

For the majority of my career, I have worked with people who have restricted their food and/or have tried to shrink and contain their body in some form or another. I have been the only person of color in a room full of eating disorder clinicians more times than I can count. Eating disorder conferences are a sea of thin white women with straight hair falling just below their shoulders. Multiple times I have been approached by conference attendees who call me by some other name because they think I'm the one Black clinician they know. I am often the peppercorn in their saltshaker; I am only there via accident, but once I've settled in, I'm hard to remove. I somehow always end up in the corner, visible and obviously out of place. The eating disorder field has never been ready for me and the truths I tell when I show up. Similarly, it has never been able to support my clients. Centering those most impacted by the narratives written by white supremacy was, and continues to be, too great an ask for a field that prioritizes those who have been written to be fragile and vulnerable: thin, white, cis women.

I come to this book as an expert only of my own clinical experiences rather than an expert of evidence-based practices. In part, because I just can't. As of this writing, when I look in the National Library of Medicine database, also known as PubMed, and type in "eating disorders" and "Black women," only ten results from the last five years appear, and only one study of Black women exclusively, while the majority compare Black women to white women, who are clearly defined as the norm or default sample population. Meanwhile, there are 8,173 results for "eating disorders." I don't think it is ethical to say that we're providing "evidence-based" care to Black women with eating disorders when they are present in 0.001 percent of the research.

I also won't cite many peer-reviewed sources because the research areas and hypotheses are biased. For example, of those ten results for Black women, there were three for binge eating disorder, three for bulimia, and zero for anorexia; the other four were not specific to eating disorders in Black women. The focus on eating disorders that involve a bingeing component is consistent with this country's association of Blackness with gluttony. Researchers and institutions erase Black women from studies that don't fit with societal expectations for our bodies. So often in our society, if something hasn't been "studied," it doesn't exist. As such, one could make the argument that Black women simply don't get anorexia. When people are not assessed and diagnosed with restrictive eating disorders, they are more likely to have adverse outcomes, and it can require far more resources to support someone's recovery than had they been supported earlier. I've endured multiple eating disorder educational events during which clinicians, including Black clinicians, stick strictly to the research without critiquing the biases and discrepancies in the data collection and the results. This not only reinforces the idea that Black women only have eating disorders with an "overeating" component but also results in Black clinicians inadvertently pathologizing themselves and reinforcing their connection to gluttony.

In 2021, I was excited to attend a webinar about eating disorders among Black women in college settings hosted by two Black psychologists and eating disorder "specialists." Finally, someone was talking about the population I was most interested in! The clinicians, both of whom worked for a college counseling center, told the audience that they have observed emotional and binge eating in Black female college students, consistent with the existing research. The clinicians believe that Black women are more likely to binge eat coming to college, compared to white peers, because they witness Black men dating white women in college, specifically. They hypothesized that this leads to emotional eating from their despair. The clinicians even showed us a photo of what seemed to be a formal fraternity event with a group of Black men paired with white women. This was supposed proof of their hypothesis and how they were able to align with the academic research.

Girl, no. This reductive explanation for the presence of disordered eating in Black college-aged women is not what anyone needs. Making these conclusions not only reduces the causes of disordered eating to desiring the attention of a man but also centers men in stories about Black women's bodies. This message ignores the entire story written about Black women's bodies by white supremacy. Good thing this webinar was free. My heart was broken thinking that these were the messages the presenters were sharing with their clients and that students would contextualize their experiences such that attention from Black men would be a recovery goal. I was simultaneously disappointed that this was what the audience would think was true about the experiences of Black women with eating disorders. I couldn't help but also wonder what these clinicians thought of their own body stories, and how much of their self-worth was in the hands of Black men. Black women are not immune to taking on the narratives about our bodies that we have been told for decades.

This presentation was one example of our society's overreliance on data and "proof" to justify someone's existence. In clinical care, so often we do not allow individuals to be the experts of their own experience and to tell us what they need. Most nutrition, body weight, and Health-related data do not examine the intersections of race, socioeconomic status, trauma history, gender identity, sexuality, disability, neurodiversity, documentation status, and access to food, safe drinking water, clean air, education, employment, health care, and transportation—among many other disparities. When we consistently center thin, white, cis, non-disabled, neurotypical, and well-resourced people in our "best practices," there is no way for us to ethically incorporate "evidence" into our work, in my opinion, with people who do not have these privileged identities. Instead of best practices created to be inherently exclusionary, I will use the narratives of those around me, my clients, my friends, my family, and my colleagues, to illustrate the outcomes of body stories written through a white lens. The long-standing narratives written about Black women's bodies shape how we all navigate the world. Black women in Western society were denied the power to write our own existence into national and international discourse, and try as we might, the lens through which we view ourselves and other Black women is invariably shaped by what whiteness has demanded.

This book examines the ways in which this shows up in ourselves, in our relationships, and on our bodies. I explore the ways in which the structures and systems that govern our lives are heavily based on the stories written, by white supremacy, about our bodies. I explore and critique the contemporary solutions to the negative messages we receive about our bodies, and I make the case for a shift in how we write and read body narratives.

• • •

IN MY TRAINING TO BECOME A DIETITIAN, I DIDN'T LEARN ABOUT the structural forces, epigenetics, or toxic stress that impact the food eaten in marginalized communities. As dietitians, we're educated to believe in individual responsibility; we're taught to tell our patients to "eat healthier" and that the only barrier to doing so is their willingness. Trauma is not discussed, and dietitians are not taught how to hold the trauma for our clients.

I was taught that eating disorder treatment was best left to therapists. Dietitians could provide specific meal plans, but most of the work would happen in therapy. I didn't learn how to become an integrated member of a treatment team that includes therapy and medical and psychiatric support until I was already doing the work. Dietitians were taught the medical impacts of starving and purging via vomiting, that was it. It formed how I viewed eating disorder behaviors to have one of two presentations rather than a wide spectrum with many intersections. As training was limited, it was easy to adopt the common perception in the field that all women adopt disordered eating patterns for a sense of control and a desire for thinness, visibility, status, and the male gaze. As such, the conversation includes gay men, who are also assumed to value the male gaze. All other individuals are routinely disregarded. Eating disorders in Black women and other folks whose bodies don't conform to societal requirements are often different—and more harmful—quests. White women, by virtue of being white, are closer to this culture's racist body ideal, and therefore closer to feeling safe and seen, even as they may also hold marginalized identities. Black women will never come close to the body ideal that whiteness upholds—thin will never be thin enough to tame a Black woman's body.

This harm not only validates disordered eating for Black women but also leads to internalized anti-Blackness and shame.

I am constantly focused on how to care for bodies that are stereotyped as strong but that are, in reality, deeply vulnerable to the manifestations of white supremacy. In my practice, I help my patients contextualize how the narratives written during enslavement continue to exist today. Black women often take on the false idea that we have superhuman strength and resilience, in the meantime sacrificing our physical and mental health trying to make ourselves fit into a society that will never accept us. This replicates centuries of lacking body autonomy for Black women, of being denied agency in how we tend to our bodies.

. . .

EARLY IN MY LEARNING I WOULD HAVE APPROACHED MIA FROM A place of already knowing. I would have told her she needed to talk to her doctor about getting an eating disorder assessment. I would have created a meal plan for her and a goal of trusting her body and eating intuitively.

But today I don't.

Instead, I listen.

We discuss the influences of whiteness on her reality, and I validate her experiences. I tell her I don't have The Answer because her experience is rooted in both her lived experience and the politics of the external world.

She isn't ready to hear about this. She isn't ready to give things up. And that's okay.

A glance at the clock tells me our time is almost up, and I offer Mia a follow-up appointment. As she disappears down the hallway, I lean back against the wall and look again at *Breathe Beauty*. I let out a deep sigh and invite air down into my belly after holding it tightly in my chest. These moments never get easier. After appointments like these there's a mixture of sadness, anger, and despair that swirls within me. The first few times it happened, I teared up, at a loss for how to problem solve something with clients that was impossible to fix; fixing was something I'd been trained to do. I'd sit in silence as clients shared their trauma, knowing I couldn't change anything about the past, and wonder what my role was in these situations. I couldn't share my experiences with white colleagues in consultation because no one was experiencing what was in the room with me. The realities of living under white supremacy never get easier, but over time I've found ways to channel my energy into collective and cultural change. In 2020, I finally found other Black clinicians who did similar work and experienced the same dynamics in their office. And having clients trust me with their stories and allow me to offer support on their path to healing is my healing as well.

. . .

IN WRITING THIS BOOK I ENDEAVOR TO MAKE MY LANGUAGE AS clear as possible, and when writing about identities that aren't my own, I defer to thought leaders and community members to guide me.

I use *white supremacy* to describe the ideology that created the race-based caste system that prioritizes and protects white people and serves to destroy and demoralize all others. And I use the term *whiteness*, not as the white race but as the ways white supremacy shows up in our society and on our bodies. In this book I note the many ways whiteness is working the way it is intended. An example of it working is when white people, especially white women, take cultural criticism personally; they make it about them rather than about the structures of caste. Taking it personally distracts from the systems that uphold whiteness and lets people focus on one-to-one relationships and individual solutions to systemic problems. It means they never need to be uncomfortable with complicity and complacency under white supremacy.

To describe body size and shape, I use *thin* and *fat*. Although both terms are social constructions, fluid and situational—think "fitness," entertainment, cities, regions, communities—in this book I use these distinctions as a function of access. I use *thin* to describe people who are generally able to go shopping for clothes and find something that fits them without needing to seek out a specialty store or a different section all the way in the back. Thin people don't need seat belt extenders on airplanes and in cars and don't have to think twice about whether they can find seating wide enough and with a high enough weight capacity to hold them. In this book thinness has nothing to do with body weight because the appearance of someone's body size is how we are judged by society. I use *fat* to describe people who are told their sizes are only available online or who are unable to get clothing items from independent suppliers because having them in stock "would drive up costs on all of our merchandise." Fat students aren't able to sit in the lecture hall seating of the universities they pay to attend. Fat people are denied medical care because society abides by arbitrary cutoffs in sizes and weights for certain medical equipment like blood pressure cuffs and procedures like surgeries. Fat people who can become pregnant aren't often told that emergency contraception, other than a copper IUD, isn't as effective for them. Fat people are often preexisting symptoms in and of themselves and are denied humanity in the medical system.

Fatness is often interpreted as a moral failing, a Bad Thing. Fat activists have reclaimed *fat* as an adjective.[2] Ashleigh Shackelford states, "Fat is a descriptor in the same way that black and queer are descriptors. And fat is somewhat similar to black and queer in more than just that way; it's also a word that encompasses a marginalized identity. Yes, fat is a neutral and descriptive word, but when it's an identity, it's much more than that. To reclaim this word, or any word, is to lean into an identity as a form of revolution against fatphobia, racism, and so much more. For me, fat is a way of saying 'f*ck you.'"[3]

When referring to body weight designations, as applied by the World Health Organization and the medical-industrial complex, I use quotation marks because "underweight," "normal weight," "overweight," and "obese" are assessed by height and weight equations and do not always align with the size of our bodies. For example, "obese" people may not be fat. They also pathologize body weight, body size, and therefore people who are any measure above or below the realm of what is deemed "normal." These words are used only in the context of the medical-industrial complex.

I use both *Health* and *Healthy*, and *health* and *healthy*. I use Health and Healthy (capital *H*) as states of being and to describe the broader social agreements in the United States of what makes a good body. Health (capital *H*) is a social construction and often assumed via body type alone. Lowercase *health* and *healthy* are the medical textbook definitions, the absence of disease; healthy people go to the doctor and are told they're fine.

I use *Sick* as an identifier for those of us with chronic illnesses, those with a medical diagnosis, those who have yet to be diagnosed, and those for whom there isn't a medical diagnosis to encapsulate their experience of illness under white supremacy. I use *Sick* as an identity, a state of being. I will use *sick* (lowercase *s*) to describe a general or acute illness and in the context of the medical-industrial complex.

I use *Wellness* (capital *W*) to describe the billion-dollar industry that promises a transcendental experience of a body and the purity and morality associated with the engagement of Wellness practices. Instead of a lowercase *wellness*, I use *well-being* because it refers to a state of existence.

I use the term *marginalized* in this book. At the time of this writing some activists and educators are shifting from using *marginalized* to terms like *historically excluded* and *intentionally ignored*. I want to acknowledge this shift away and note that I have yet to find a term that I believe represents the contemporary violence of what people continue to experience in a society that has been constructed in such a way that anyone who falls outside of what whiteness requires will never be allowed to fully participate, even if they were to be included.

When I use *Black women*, I mean *every* Black woman, all sexes assigned at birth. The experiences here center Black women and you will find they may be applicable to many people whose body stories have been written by whiteness.

In my discussion of race, specifically for Brown and non-Black people of color, I am not referring to those who are assigned whiteness or who are considered to be white passing. Although I understand that people may choose to identify as a person of color, consistent with their ethnicity, family, heritage, and political identity, I refer to race as an assignment. I understand that race is a social construct and fluid, as US history has shown, so I am not referring to people who are protected and shielded by their ability to be seen as white. For the purposes of this book, those who are assigned whiteness are a part of the dominant caste. They may share cultural experiences with Black and Brown people, but they do not carry the same flashcard of how they are to be treated, and thus have different experiences navigating the structure and systems that organize the existence of the colonized country that is called the United States.

Most of this book takes place around 2020–2021. It was a time during which Black women were noticed, perhaps in ways we never will be again. And even then, our Blackness was viewed through the lens of whiteness. In 2020, people were discussing the need for Black women to lead. There was an increase in anti-racism training and internal DEI promotions were suddenly trendy. Our focus was drawn to the new bright shiny object, the solution. "Learning" was pitched as The Way to getting out of a caste system, yet came with no expectation of "doing." Meanwhile, those of us who need justice and liberation are expected to witness white people, and those with close proximity to whiteness learn about their privilege. We're expected to take a *wait and see* approach to whether this "learning" ever translates to doing.

Nationally, white author Robin DiAngelo's book *White Fragility: Why It's So Hard for White People to Talk About Racism* was fast becoming a best seller. White fragility, as a concept, is convenient; it provides a reason for people to excuse themselves from hard conversations and not have to sit with discomfort. When we label someone's defensiveness and lack of willingness to sit with discomfort as *fragility*, we distance them from the harm they have caused. We attribute the harm to their whiteness rather than their lack of ability to do better, be accountable, or simply be a decent human being. White fragility, as a concept, upholds the belief that whiteness is delicate, frail, and needs protection. It perpetuates the idea that Blackness, inherently the opposite, is strong, resilient, and won't experience pain.

The stories written about all bodies, from their race and shade to their size and shape, from what they should eat to how to do so, have historically been written by medical doctors, researchers, professors, and religious leaders. For centuries, white men with some version of credentials and, increasingly, white women with the same have been those who have constructed the narrative of a "good body." This group of people has dictated which bodies follow the rules and, consequently, which do not. It constructed the parameters for bodies that uphold the historically Anglo-Saxon values of purity and morality at the foundations of many Western societies. The pure, moral, rule-abiding body has never, ever been a Black woman's. The narratives about Black women's bodies are always juxtaposed with those of a better body, historically a white woman's body. Fast-forward to the end of the twentieth century and then a quarter into the twenty-first, and white women are dominating the narrative about Health, Wellness, and body positivity. These constructs are no accident; they are by design.

This book makes the case for a cultural rewriting, something that does not fall directly upon the shoulders of those most impacted by our current system of caste but on a society as a whole. In their book *Belly of the Beast: The Politics of Anti-Fatness as Anti-Blackness*, Da'Shaun L. Harrison notes that "systems and institutions are maintained by power but are created first through an idea. At the root, liberation must mean cultural revolution as well as a deconstruction of the sociopolitical institutions that hold these systems in place."[4] Everyone needs to participate in this revolution. This book makes the case for a cultural revolution that centers and prioritizes Black women, those who have been most impacted by the patriarchal, capitalistic, caste-based society in the United States. The *ideas* about Black women and our caste system need to change.

This book is specifically for Black women. To end the pathologizing and problematizing of our bodies, for us to stop placing ownership of whiteness onto our bodies. May you see yourself in a book about bodies in a way that hasn't been done before. May you see that none of it has been your fault. It's been by design. The world was not constructed to take in your abundance.

Having a body is hard. Hopefully, the conversations you find here will help you make sense of your experience in a way that lets you live a bit freer.

This book makes the case for a new narrative and demands that we all celebrate Black Joy.

PART 1

"LIVE, LAUGH, LOVE"

chapter one

It Isn't Diet Culture, It's White Supremacy

IN 2020, BLACK WOMEN WERE NOTICED IN A WAY THAT WE hadn't been before, with interest that would subside as quickly as it had peaked. The same year also brought a shift in the eating disorder field that I hadn't seen coming. The murder of Black people by the police and a global pandemic did what no Black clinician had yet been able to do: bring our existence into conversations (albeit peripherally) about food and bodies. It took horrific events for Black lives to matter in my field.

Many of my white eating disorder clinician colleagues took to social media in late spring of 2020. Having never done so prior, they now had Things To Say about racial injustice. The whiplash from messages like *All Bodies Are Good Bodies* and *Just Eat the Cake* to *Black Lives Matter* and the understanding that "wow, systemic

racism is still a thing!" were profound. During these murder in-
vestigations, my white eating disorder clinician colleagues were
lauded for something that my Black colleagues and I had been
doing for years, much to the disdain of the dietetics-, eating disorder–, and weight stigma–focused communities, who weren't able
to sit with the discomfort that our truths provided.

• • •

SHORTLY AFTER MY ENTRANCE INTO THE EATING DISORDER FIELD, I
connected with Bay Area fat-positive communities that were focused
on addressing weight stigma in the medical model. The groups
were also advocating for size-inclusive eating disorder care. The
community members were mostly middle-aged, white, fat women
who were very economically privileged; I was the only melanated
individual among them. When I inquired about why I was the only
person of color at the literal and figurative table, I'd get told:

"Oh, so-and-so used to come!" and

"So-and-so was here a few months back!" and

"Have you met [that one other Black woman who had been in-
volved]? You two should connect!"

Nevertheless, I continued to show up as the conversations about
weight stigma in the medical model were essential for my clients'
care.

Just after the murder of Eric Garner at the hands of New York
City police in 2014, I decided to talk with these colleagues about
the intersections of fatness and Blackness. They had solely focused
on the ways weight stigma impacted them as individuals, and some
had denied they inherently had privilege, even putting *privilege* in

quotes to reference what I was discussing. I thought that Garner's murder, surely, would be the moment they could no longer deny the need to have more complex discussions about fatness. How could they not connect Garner's Blackness and fatness to the idea that he was a threat? He was overpoliced because he was Black, and his death was not ruled a murder because his fatness was blamed as a "contributing factor" for the reason he couldn't breathe. I took a deep breath and brought up the intersections to my colleagues. Before I could finish the pitch to have more complex conversations about anti-fat violence I was cut off—

"This isn't about *that*, Jessica."

"This isn't the oppression olympics." They told me that when we complicate the movement with these topics, "it's always a race to the bottom."

I was shocked.

I shouldn't have been. Whiteness was working.

Seven years later, in the summer of 2020, it was folks from these same communities who now were speaking up about their Learning and had Things To Say.

. . .

WHILE FOLKS WERE LEARNING IN 2020, I WAS TRYING NOT TO have emotional meltdowns every time I checked the news and social media. I was trying to keep my face together while talking to my clients. At the same time, there was a flood of requests from white clinicians with podcasts and platforms inviting me and other Black colleagues to be guests on their shows and on Instagram Live. We were asked to talk about the racial trauma our clients experience in eating disorder recovery and about our own trauma in the field. We were offered nothing but "exposure" in return; last time I checked, exposure doesn't pay bills.

Eating disorder therapist Alishia McCullough and I had been following each other on Instagram for a couple months and had sent messages of solidarity back and forth before ending up on a Zoom consultation call with eating disorder clinicians who had responded to the pandemic shutdown of eating disorder support groups with a sense of urgency. The clinicians had organized meal groups via Instagram Live and eventually realized that they could have done some things differently from the start to prioritize marginalized clients and clinicians' labor. They invited my feedback, and I was so relieved to see Alishia's face when I logged on; it was great to speak truth to power alongside another Black woman.

About 3.7 minutes after the consultation ended, Alishia and I were talking on the phone. We debriefed about how white supremacy culture was on full display in the meeting and in our field. We realized that we were having parallel experiences three thousand miles apart. I told her that for my last interview request I'd asked to be paid. I had done too many interviews that had resulted in my exhaustion having tried to convince the hosts that, even though the current frameworks and principles worked for them, I had seen them backfire for my clients and community. The high-profile host declined to pay me. Alishia told me that she'd received an invite for her free labor from the same host. We discussed how saying yes to these invitations without any compensation (financial or as a part of promoting, say, a book) perpetuates the idea that we're able to be used for our labor only to bolster the social capital of white women who collect us. In 2020, Ahmaud Arbery, Breonna Taylor, bird-watcher Christian Cooper, and George Floyd had prime real estate in our minds alongside a global pandemic. We were emotionally spent and were sitting silently in the shadows watching our white colleagues get praised for "calling attention to these issues." Their messages, often recycled from content creators of color, and watered down, weren't what our clients needed and weren't what we needed as clinicians.

On that call, we decided that on June 1, 2020, we would challenge our nearly three thousand combined Instagram followers to Amplify Melanated Voices on social media. We wrote, "Social justice conversations consistently center white people's narratives and make them feel like the 'good white person' or the 'woke white person.'" And, "The language and offerings are often appropriated from the lived experiences of Black and Brown folks and is [sic] then used to make a profit and increase [the white person's] social capital." Additionally, Black and Brown folks "go without credit and payment, and are pushed further into the margins of social justice work as white audiences continue to center themselves."

We then asked our Instagram followers to "Look at your favorite white social media content creators, they most likely have thousands/millions of followers and endorsements. Meanwhile accounts of Black and Brown people are being policed, reported, and targeted by trolls while their work is stolen and repackaged by these top names on social media. . . . We challenge you to Amplify Melanated Voices this week, and silence the white narrative by muting the accounts of the white people [they] follow and sharing content from melanated creators in their stories, with credit." Our followers were mostly those in the body political community; we wanted to know whether for just one week people could live without being told to love their body and be comfortable eating a cookie.

We were sure we'd lose followers and be able to point to this as an example of the field not being able to have hard conversations. However, it was 2020, and people were looking for Things To Do during the racial reckoning (that wasn't). We received an enormous amount of feedback and offers for collaboration. I ended up with over one hundred thousand Instagram followers and finally made connections with Black eating disorder clinicians.

One comment on my thread of Instagram posts about the challenge stuck with me. A Black woman asked me to stop calling it a challenge for everyone to mute white voices. I replied, "I wish it wasn't."

• • •

THOUGH AMPLIFY MELANATED VOICES TOOK JUST WEEKS TO plan with Alishia, it was over a decade in the making for me. I became a registered dietitian at the end of 2006.* Soon after I passed my dietitian exam and became registered, I worked in a diabetes management clinic in Eugene, Oregon, before starting grad school and a practicum placement with the athletic department at the University of Oregon. People often think that my eating disorder clinical experience started in athletes, but it wasn't until I had my first "real job" working at a student health center in Oregon that I

---

* Registered Dietitian Nutritionists—dietitians, for short—are medical clinicians who are hired in medical facilities. We are different from those who are nutritionists. Dietitians undergo a didactic program, complete a dietetic internship, and sit for a standardized exam. Nutritionists are not required to do any of these things. Nutritionists can call themselves such at birth; there are no criteria, no exam. Nutritionists are not qualified to provide medical care.

had a high volume of clients with eating disorders. I was absolutely unenthused to work with people who didn't want to eat food.

I was a first-generation college student who didn't have dinner table conversations about choosing college majors or what income I could expect from each field; the only specific guidance I received was that I needed to finish college. One day, while filling out online college applications and clicking the "undeclared" boxes, my mom asked if I knew I could major in nutrition. I had not, and learned I could make a living by talking to people all day about eating food. It was the late nineties and people were still eating SnackWell's and were told that we could eat only one egg per day and that trans fats were the biggest threat to our lives. My nutrition knowledge at the time was limited to scare tactics and subtractive messages from public health and the media, but nonetheless I wanted to talk about food. Fast-forward ten years and my primary job duty was to talk to people who wanted anything but to talk with me about food, let alone eat it. Womp. Frankly speaking, I was not a good eating disorder clinician that first year, perhaps for the first two. I bought books and consulted with therapists, but those resources never went beyond the commonly held beliefs that eating disorders stemmed from "wanting to control something," and the only clinical examples provided were thin white girls and women who were afraid to gain weight.

A year or two into that job, I started working with two queer women, one of whom was Indigenous, the other Mexican, who were restricting food in order to shrink their bodies. Both weren't "underweight" and the medical team was flummoxed. The physiological impacts of starvation were clear from their lab results, heart rate, blood pressure, and mental health, yet our clients' bodies didn't reflect as much. The medical team didn't know what was happening and this situation certainly hadn't been in the books I was reading. Throughout my clinical practice, I had known that counting calories wasn't useful, and now I saw firsthand that calories in–calories out was simply false. The cornerstone of my nutrition education had been a lie, and I needed to start again at square one.

Shortly after starting with those clients, their medical provider and I attended a free training by a nationally recognized medical doctor who specialized in eating disorder care. He was speaking at a venue near Eugene, Oregon, while promoting his network of treatment centers, one of which was nearby. The treatment center was offering free continuing education to the medical providers in the area who wanted to come hear the physician talk and advertise his center. There were over a hundred people in attendance, most of whom were women. My colleagues and I were looking for guidance on treating eating disorder patients, having found we didn't know what to do when faced with someone who didn't fit the literal textbook definition of an eating disorder.

The physician had a PowerPoint presentation that included research and best practices. He shared his treatment center's protocol for weight restoration, which involved standardized weight gain goals and timelines. He used calculations like "ideal body weight" that assume people are "underweight" to begin with and need to gain enough weight to be "ideal." His protocol was based on research done decades ago on mostly middle-aged white men, not based on a client's own typical weight when not attempting to shrink or contain their body.* I was still new to eating disorder care and didn't know

---

* Body mass index (BMI). So much fatphobic and racist nonsense to unpack in the development of that measure—that's a tomorrow problem.

why there were such arbitrary cutoffs for what recovery got to look like, but he was the expert!

When it came time for questions, my hand was the first to shoot into the air. After answering others' questions, he got around to me.

"How can clinicians gauge recovery progress when a client is already at a 'normal' weight or 'overweight'?" I asked.

He gave me a skeptical look and replied, "Those scenarios aren't possible," dismissing my question and keeping it moving.

The doctor with whom I had attended and I exchanged confused glances. Were we just wrong about what we were seeing? She raised her hand.

"No, I'm a doctor and I'm seeing these patients as well," she said when called upon.

Apparently, this was too much for the speaker. He squared up to the podium and addressed the whole crowd. "In our Colorado facility we treat *serious* eating disorder cases. I don't know what is happening with your patients, but I am talking about girls who are *actually* sick."

Message received. We were clearly derailing the conversation. We all needed to get back to talking about the girls who have *real* eating disorders, because ours clearly do not. The end. My colleague and I didn't get a chance to say that one of our clients needed to be at a treatment center but that she was denied insurance coverage because she wasn't "underweight" and that consequently she had increased her self-harm and restrictive behaviors so that she could become *actually* sick and granted coverage. Through his gaslighting of our experience, I began to put the picture together of who, both clients and clinicians, was to be taken seriously and valued by the eating disorder elites and who was to be dismissed. He confirmed to the audience who mattered. It was my first introduction to the lengths the eating disorder establishment will go to reinforce the idea that thin white girls and women are those who get eating disorders and deserve care. I also saw how far the eating disorder elites would go to keep those whose bodies don't signal frailty and oftentimes signal fear, out.

Over the next decade, as I embedded myself into the section of the eating disorder community that was fat-positive and believed that if someone was hungry they should eat food, I saw hollow attempts to address the protection of thinness and whiteness with statements like "eating disorders don't discriminate" and the touting of statistics of the rates of eating disorders among folks of color, queer folks, and "overweight" folks. But the field stopped at these declarations. There was no plan, no commitment, no critique of frameworks and no accountability to do better. There was absolutely no commitment to change anything within the eating disorder establishment, no discussions about changing treatment modalities and assessments or recruiting clinicians with a variety of lived experiences. It was business as usual. The eating disorder field was broken.

. . .

TEN YEARS LATER, IN THE LATE TWENTY-TEENS, THERE WERE NEW voices attempting to change the culture and conversation about dieting and eating disorders, most of whom were thin white women. Christy Harrison, a registered dietitian with a master of public health degree, was credited with transforming the eating disorder field via her podcast *Food Psych*. I hadn't heard of Harrison until a 2019 eating disorder conference at which she was discussed as a recovery celebrity. In 2020, among a barrage of fatphobic, pithy sayings like "Quarantine 15" and others' declarations about using the extra time they had during the pandemic shutdown to overexercise and stop eating food, people were looking for the antidote. Harrison's 2019 book *Anti-Diet: Reclaim Your Time, Money, Well-Being, and Happiness Through Intuitive Eating* was a sought-after resource. In her book, she draws connections among capitalism, morality, food, and thinness. She is also credited with coining the term *diet culture*, a system of beliefs that

> Worships thinness and equates it to health and moral virtue. . . . Promotes weight loss as a means of attaining higher status. . . . Demonizes certain ways of eating while elevating others. . . . Oppresses people who don't match up with its supposed picture of "health."

She writes that "you can spend your whole life thinking you're irreparably broken just because you don't look like the impossibly thin 'ideal.'" And that paying close attention to our food choices "distracts us from our pleasure, our purpose, and our power." I saw more and more calls on social media and from colleagues to "dismantle diet culture!" and become body positive and eat intuitively. I heard from new dietitians that becoming "anti-diet" clinicians was going to be the fix the eating disorder field so desperately needed. Harrison is credited with popularizing intuitive eating as the solution to our collective concerns about eating and drawing attention in the eating disorder field to the science that body weight is not an indicator of health and to the ridiculous applications of BMI.

On the surface, I was glad that the truths fat folks had been telling us for years about their experiences of weight stigma and anti-fat violence had finally made it into mainstream dialogues. I heard, anecdotally, that fat folks were grateful for this too. I was also sad. It took a thin white woman with social capital for the eating disorder elites to hear the truth about weight science. Of course it did. She fit the demographic of people who were prioritized in the field; she mattered.

The year 2020 also brought renewed interest in Dr. Sabrina Strings's *Fearing the Black Body: The Racial Origins of Fat Phobia*, published in 2019. Dr. Strings, a thin Black associate professor at the University of California, Irvine, compiled centuries' worth of literature to carefully construct the argument that the Western world's vilification of fatness is one outcome of anti-Blackness. During a period of increased conversations about race and proclamations of allyship in the summer of 2020, her work was garnering new attention in the eating disorder field. In her book, she details the function of food restriction as a tool for white women to achieve and maintain both thinness and superiority over Black women. Withholding food was primarily in service of socially constructing clear distinctions between themselves and the hedonism of Blackness.

Dr. Strings detailed the engineering efforts of white men to link fatness with Black women and then craft the narrative that fatness needed fearing. The success at constructing this association has bound Black women's bodies to fear ever since. Strings details the story of Sarah (or Saartjie) Baartman, born in the late eighteenth century as an enslaved woman in Cape Town, South Africa. At the turn of the nineteenth century, Baartman was trafficked from her homeland and forced to be on display in London in such venues as Piccadilly Circus.[1] She was an exhibition; people came to gawk at her large body, especially her buttocks. People paid to objectify her, to gape at the spectacle that Black women's bodies were literally billed to be. Strings writes that the exploitation of Baartman "helped make fatness an intrinsically black, and implicitly off-putting, form of feminine embodiment in the European scientific and popular imagination."[2]

Centuries after the objectification of Baartman, the narrative of Black women's uncontained nature continues to construct artificial differences between white and Black women. In the late 1800s, if white women remained thin, they could corner the market on virtue in the States. Strings writes about an 1896 *Harper's Bazaar* article by an unnamed author who tells the reader, "Stoutness, corpulence, and surplusage of flesh are never desirable except among African savages." In this article, as well as in others from that time period, we see that white women were writing contemporary narratives about what makes a Good Woman's body. They tied a smaller body to the purity of the white, specifically Anglo-Saxon, race. At the time, whiteness endeavored to define what made a pure woman, particularly in her deviation from the fat, savage African. The *Harper's Bazaar* author also teased out the connection between immorality and eating habits. These philosophies set the course for the Western world to use body size and food choices to draw a distinction between those whose bodies follow the rules and those who do not. One can see the connection between these messages and the impacts felt more than one century later. Society continues to assign fatness as a distinct marker of gluttony and ties it to Blackness. Over hundreds of years, our society has socially constructed both race and fatness. We use these agreed-upon constructions to both demonize

Black women and keep us all obedient by perpetually engaging in attempts to shrink ourselves and practice restraint while eating.

Both Harrison and Strings were writing new narratives. Both gave the eating disorder field a new lens through which we could see the body stories of Black women. One author simplified our experiences to desiring the thin ideal, the other gave centuries of historical context to the reasons that Black women may want to constrain our bodies to comply with what whiteness demands, particularly for survival.

. . .

IN LATE SUMMER AND FALL OF 2020, THE EATING DISORDER FIELD decided it could no longer disregard the critiques leveled from Black clinicians. It also, like most other establishments, took a cue from popular culture and decided to squeeze discussions of race into conversations clinicians were already having. I was invited to multiple webinars to discuss the disparities Black folks face when seeking eating disorder treatment, and in each one, the concession made was that diet culture has *roots* in racism. There was integration of both Strings's and Harrison's work, but it was clear that one argument was bolstering the other.

I continue to hear this sentiment. In addition to my colleagues, social media influencers make this claim as well. Matt McGorry, an actor and body image influencer with over a million Instagram followers, most known for playing Asher Millstone on *How to Get Away with Murder* and John Bennet in *Orange Is the New Black*, shared that he read both *Fearing the Black Body* and *Anti-Diet*. His analysis was that diet culture and fatphobia make up "a hydra-headed beast, and that race is but one tentacle." After reading *both* books, he drew the conclusion that diet culture is The Problem with how bodies are viewed in society, and that white supremacy is just one of the contributors to diet culture and fatphobia. Nope. When we relegate racism to "the roots" of diet culture, we send the message that, sure, racism may have played a role in the development of the quest to shrink our bodies, but if we are able to dismantle diet culture, then racism will, by proxy, be destroyed as well. That's not it. Diet culture is not the driving force behind the ways our bodies are under surveillance by society.

McGorry is not alone. There are similar lacking analyses among clinicians and in fat-positive spaces. I've heard "Fat is the last acceptable prejudice" in multiple settings, including the previously mentioned 2019 eating disorder conference. For some people, weight stigma is the only prejudice they face, and it can feel like anti-fatness is the only culturally condoned injustice to them and thin white allies agree. I can see how dismantling diet culture would seem the primary goal for those who are unwilling to engage with the narratives written about others' bodies. But for those of us who continue to see the hunting and execution of Black people by law enforcement and white nationalists, the ever-growing ways trans people's existence is legislated and used as political theater, how what someone does with their own uterus is criminalized, and the many other ways bodies experience violence, it does not feel like fat is the last acceptable prejudice. For most of us, dismantling diet culture will not make it safer for us to exist in society.

"I believe dieting is oppressive," she told me. During a 2021 call about the difference between structural weight stigma and break-room talk about Weight Watchers (now WW), a thin, cis, white eating disorder therapist I worked with told me and my colleague that she believes that dieting, in and of itself, is oppressive. As if, somehow, caloric suppression itself is oppression. Although engaging in caloric deprivation may absolutely feel distressing and perhaps like the hardest thing someone has ever endured, it is not unjust, authoritative, systemic, or structural. Harrison's book reinforced my coworker's theory. She says, "And when you think about the levels of stress we experience from living in diet culture, it's clear that trauma is exactly what we're dealing with. Just like any other oppressive system, diet culture is traumatic."[3] The idea that diet culture in and of itself is oppressive and traumatic invites those with relative privilege to take the opportunity to speak as authorities of body liberation because we're all subject to societal pressures to engage in intentional weight loss.

The rallying cry to dismantle diet culture is a simple solution to a collective pursuit to wither our bodies when there are far greater and consequential systems at play. WW is not the primary reason that Black women are told they are too much. The worship of thinness in our society is not the primary threat to Black women's existence, and I don't believe diet culture is the primary reason that Black women seek to shrink and contain our bodies.

When dieting and the culture of dieting are oppressive and traumatic, messages of "liberation" get to be:

"All food is guilt free!"
"Just eat the damn cake!"

"Food has no moral value!"

"Your food choices say nothing about who you are as a person!"

"Live, Laugh, Love!"

AND MANY PEOPLE STAY HERE, WHERE IT IS SAFE, BELIEVING THAT these messages are the radical transformation that everyone needs. Staying in a place where eating cake is liberation protects those who directly benefit from upholding whiteness and thinness from having to address the far greater and more complicated legacy of white supremacy and its contribution to anti-fatness. Having simple, narrow conversations keeps people comfortable, secure even, in being able to talk about bodies in ways that are limited to dieting and not about anti-Blackness, the legacy of enslavement in the United States, and colonialism across the globe.

I need more complexity and depth in the conversations that I have about bodies. I need something that extends beyond the attainment of the thin ideal. I need something that acknowledges that, in fact, social capital is assigned to bodies and foods, and that #allbodiesaregoodbodies and #allfoodsaregoodfoods dismiss lived experiences. In 2020, I started talking about the intersections of white supremacy, food, and bodies with my clients. Most of them were grateful for the context. For some, it was too much; they were looking for a dietitian who wouldn't complicate their recovery by adding body politics and historical context to the conversation. And that's absolutely okay, anti-diet dietitians are readily available.

When white women's experiences are centered in stories about food and bodies, we see second-wave feminism's continued influence. Everyone's body liberation becomes tied to those with much of the privilege and societal capital. We get dramatically incomplete visions, like this one written by white fat activist Jes Baker in her 2018 book *Landwhale: On Turning Insults into Nicknames, Why Body Image Is Hard, and How Diets Can Kiss My Ass*: "Liberation is freedom from *all* outside expectations, even our own. Liberation is not having to love your body all the time. Liberation is not asking permission to be included in society's ideal of beauty. Liberation is bucking the concept of beauty as currency altogether. Liberation is recognizing the systemic issues that surround us and acknowledging that perhaps we're not able to fix them all on our own. Liberation is personally giving ourselves permission to live life."[4]

In these contexts, liberation is connected to love and beauty, not to safety and survival. Systemic issues are regarded as background noise, and we're supported if we're able to tune it out.

Some of us do not have permission to just *live life* whenever we decide to do so. We're not able to Live, Laugh, Love on our way to "choose happiness." Many of us face the reality of intentional extinction. We're hunted by those claiming to "serve and protect" and those who see us as both inconvenient and deplorable. We avoid certain streets, former sundown towns, living in neighborhoods where the police will be called when we lock ourselves out and use resources, including word of mouth, to find safer places to visit and to stay. Laws are wielded as weapons to overturn voting access, make it okay for someone to drive over us at a protest, or deny us both affirming and lifesaving medical care. For us, the systemic issues are The Problem. Full Stop.

The erasure of Black women from the narratives about body liberation is by design. All of the systems that uphold the status quo of colonized nations in the Western world, and even more that are specific to the United States, work in the ways they're supposed to. Things are going according to plan. Whiteness is working in the way it needs to in order to persist and perpetuate the idea that white women are frail and in need of tending.

Black women don't need race to be a root, a tentacle, or any appendage of diet culture. Dismantling diet culture still won't make it safer for us to leave the house, even if it makes us, somehow, feel better about our bodies. We need systemic and structural changes in society and for our culture to rewrite the meaning assigned to phenotype.

We don't need to reimagine diet culture to include Black women's voices. Deciding to allow us a seat at a table that wasn't built with our existence in mind never accomplishes what we need it to. Black women are the table. Black women need to lead conversations about body liberation and dismantling white supremacy.

People say that this is such a big undertaking; reconstructing a field and a society seems impossible. Yes. And if we can manufacture a vaccine in a matter of months to get back to capitalism, and if one sea turtle with a straw up its nose (or nostril—do turtles have noses?) can result in an overnight countrywide ban on plastic straws, we can Do Hard Things. And. It will take a redistribution of power and a willingness to be wrong. We need a new table to construct a cultural narrative. I believe in us.

• • •

BLACK WOMEN NEGOTIATE OUR EXISTENCE DAILY. WE DECIDE how much to give and how much to withhold. We decide when to exert agency and autonomy over our bodies when it is, and has been, historically denied.

We do what we need to be seen.

To be heard.

Black women will always find ways to survive, even if it kills us in the process.

chapter two

Special Aliens Who Can Heal the World!: Resilience

ALFWAY THROUGH 2021, SAM SANDERS, THEN THE HOST OF NPR's *It's Been a Minute* podcast, provided an epic summation of 2020: "So much of the last year or two of activism and internet discourse has been: Support Black women! Believe Black women! Black women will save us! Black women are the future! Black women are special aliens that can heal the world!"

Whew!

From social justice communities to the business sector, Black women were billed as the key to this nation's success.

In August of 2020, *Forbes* ran an article titled "When Black Women Lead, We All Win."[1] In it, the author writes: "Black women's leadership isn't just about their strength and perseverance. It's about how consistently they show up and fight for the common good. Whether Black women are narrowing the wealth gap, fighting for free and fair elections or gearing up to assume one of the highest offices in the nation, when Black women lead, we all win." Facts. Black women have been doing this work for centuries. We show up and prioritize those who are least supported by capitalism and white supremacy. Black women are often referred to as the "backbone of the Democratic Party."[2]

That October, CNN profiled twenty-nine-year-old Wendy Caldwell-Liddell, who founded Mobilize Detroit, about her work–life balance. "Wendy Caldwell-Liddell is in a race against time, all the time. She is racing to wrap up her job as a grant-writing consultant. She is racing to get her 10-year-old son logged in to start remote learning at home since a case of coronavirus shut down his school. She is racing to drive her two-year-old daughter over to grandma's house for daycare. But now on top of that, three times a week, 29-year-old Caldwell-Liddell is racing to get Detroit voters, especially the black community, to, in her words, 'wake up.' . . . [She is] a one-woman canvassing machine in downtown Detroit . . . fighting against what she says is an apathy within the community toward politics."[3]

The United States can always count on Black women to put aside our own needs. What others call "work–life balance" is anything but.

• • •

THE 2020 PANDEMIC PROVIDED A COLLECTIVE PAUSE IN THE United States. Events were canceled. Many of us were home all day, every day. Dogs were grateful for the 24/7 attention; cats were likely annoyed. The sounds of children's voices, baby cries, and leaf blowers in meetings were a part of everyday life. People were reaching into the depths of their television streaming. *Animal Crossing* was the primary pandemic soundtrack for at least the first four months. People were constantly refreshing their social media. All were strategies to distract from constant streams of information about COVID rates, death, and chronic isolation. The video of George Floyd's murder elicited visceral reactions and made it virtually impossible to claim color blindness any longer. We were in a four-year, one-way relationship with someone whose love language was lying in 280 characters or less, and both our global reputation and our sanity were left hanging by a frayed puppet string in the hands of a Fanta-hued media personality. Many cite Trump and the brutal murder of George Floyd by Minneapolis police as the catalysts to make them see the impacts of systemic racism in the country. With the collective timeout that the pandemic provided, we had time to reflect on this country and how it operates. Many realized that the United States would be better off if white men were not in charge.

Late that year, everyone who hadn't yet fallen in love with Stacey Abrams and her collaborators in the New Georgia Project did so. If you didn't know, in 2020 you knew the power of Black women. And with good reason; Abrams, a lawyer who served in the Georgia House of Representatives from 2011 to 2017, and her team turned Georgia blue in the 2020 presidential election. They also changed the balance in the US Senate, giving Democrats the tie-breaking vote on legislation. She was credited with saving the United States, and really the world, from four more years of a

Donald Trump presidency. She really is one of those special aliens who can heal the world! Social media was full of messages like this one: "Yesss Stacey Abrams!!!! All that you endured was for this momentous moment!! Thank you!! God always has a plan." People were fans. But would it last?

As much as the conversation was driven by Black women's leadership, I believe it was something more complex that made Black women the heroes of 2020. I believe that when this country was in the midst of a global pandemic, economic uncertainty, housing crises, collective trauma, and nationwide grieving, Black women were naturally the individuals to whom this country turned to soothe them and help solve their problems. Promoting the magic of Black women in 2020 was a collective, subconscious way of looking to Black women to clean up the mess that whiteness created and provide the warmth needed for a grieving country at the same time.

• • •

The narratives of Black women are four hundred years in the making.

In *Caste*, Wilkerson details a myriad of ways that we came to believe the lie that whiteness is a superior race in this country. Dehumanization and stigmatization were two such tools that were integral to the development of our racial hierarchy and to overcoming the obvious cognitive dissonance that assigning personhood to one woman and not another based on pigmentation would require: Wilkerson describes dehumanization as "a war against truth . . . and it does not happen by accident." She argues that dehumanization quarantines the out-group "from the masses you choose to elevate" and "it program[s] everyone, even some of the targets of dehumanization, to no longer believe what their eyes can see, to no longer trust their own thoughts."[4]

Black women were not seen to share experiences with their white counterparts. White women were written as frail, in need of protection and rest, while Black women were cast as laborers, both in the field and in the home. Black people needed to be written as less than human, to be The Other. To fight the instinct that Black people shared humanity, there were a variety of stories written about Black women and their bodies. Three of the best documented are the Sapphire, the Jezebel, and the Mammy.

Ferris State University's Jim Crow Museum describes the Sapphire as "rude, loud, malicious, stubborn, and overbearing." This is the familiar trope of the Angry Black Woman (ABW), popular in the entertainment industry. "She is tart-tongued and emasculating, one hand on a hip and the other pointing and jabbing (or arms akimbo), violently and rhythmically rocking her head."[5]

The same museum describes the Jezebel "as lascivious by nature . . . seductive, alluring, worldly, beguiling, tempting, and lewd. Historically, white women, as a category, were portrayed as models of self-respect, self-control, and modesty—even sexual purity, but black women were often portrayed as innately promiscuous, even predatory."[6] Megan Thee Stallion and Cardi B in their 2020 collaboration "WAP" are excellent examples of Black women who have been assigned Jezebel status. The internet had Thoughts about their collaboration on "WAP," a rap song in which they make clear that they enjoy having sex.[7] The two were vilified for talking about sex even though male rappers and hip-hop artists have been doing it for decades. Many of us remember singing along to Ginuwine's nineties hit "Pony" in the backseat of our parents' car. "If you're horny let's do it / Ride it, my pony / My saddle's waiting / Come and jump on it." Fellow rapper Snoop Dogg felt called to address the song: "Let's have some . . . intimacy where he wants to find out rather than you telling him."[8] The rapper has his share of explicit and misogynistic lyrics, including in songs like "Ain't No Fun," in which he makes it very clear that he wants what he wants, yet made time to tell Black women how to do their job.

Both Megan Thee Stallion and Cardi B are rewriting the narrative for how Black female performers create their art.

Mammy is the narrative that I find most complicated and complex. The 2018 exhibit "Beyond Mammy, Jezebel, and Sapphire: Reclaiming Images of Black Women" features nine artists and their images of Black women alongside commentary about the three stereotypes of Black women. It describes the Mammy as "the fiercely independent, portly, desexualized domestic who was every white person's favorite grandmother. This depiction of Black women often presented mammy as more nurturing and loyal to the white family who she faithfully served than she was to her own kin."[9] She endured.

Hattie McDaniel famously won an Oscar for her role as a maid in *Gone With the Wind*; she was thought to steal the show multiple times as Mammy. It was a typecast character she played seventy-three additional times in her career. Seventy years after her award, comedian Mo'Nique won an Oscar for her role in *Precious*. The comedian wore white gardenias in her hair, as McDaniel had done when accepting her own award, and addressed the audience: "I want to thank Miss Hattie McDaniel, for enduring all she had to, so I would not have to."[10]

Jessie Parkhurst Guzman (1898–1996), an academic and historian educated at Howard University and Columbia University, compiled a variety of resources, including first-person accounts, to paint a full picture of the historical stereotype of the Black woman as Mammy, referred to specifically as the Black Mammy by those who found comfort in her presence. She found that "what we know of the 'Black Mammy' has been recorded mainly by those whom she nursed as children." Parkhurst Guzman's twenty-two-page essay, "The Role of the Black Mammy in the Plantation Household," published in the *Journal of Negro History* in 1938, details the role a Mammy played in the family and her essentialness to the plantation household. She captured forty-six descriptors of the Black Mammy that "indicate a first-hand and personal knowledge of her, which became standardized and institutionalized by sentiment." The adjectives fell into four general categories: *warmth, smart, hardworking, loyal* and specifically included "neither apish nor servile." The essay paints a picture of a woman who was dearly beloved by those she nurtured, yet whose children could be sold to settle a bet and whose real name was often unknown: "it was a matter of no significance."[11]

Enslaved Black women literally raised this country. They were required to invest in a capitalistic endeavor that was actively engaged in their extinction. They were selfless in their work, and this depiction, along with the others, has been embedded into our social conditioning. These narratives about Black women persist: we're still valued primarily for our labor and expected to nurture those most protected by whiteness and to clean up the messes they leave behind. And as these narratives persist, so do we. We have persevered in spite of the stories written about us. We've survived the lies constructed about us and we have thrived in a country that wants us dead; we're strong, we're magic, we're special aliens.

The expectations of Black women also persist. Mammy is expected to labor for the greater good and enjoy doing so at the same time. She is happy to give away a part of herself so that others might gain comfort, peace, knowledge, education, enlightenment, etcetera. She may have traded in her apron for a Birkin or a briefcase, but the expectations are the same. Today we call the ability to push beyond what is natural, to forgo our own needs and to prioritize those of the dominant caste, resilience. We say that Black women are resilient as if it were a choice rather than an assignment and a tool of survival: the strong Black woman.

. . .

Find a job you enjoy doing, and you will never have to work a day in your life.
—ATTRIBUTED TO CONFUCIUS, MARK TWAIN, AND OTHERS

Lol. Never, ever have I heard a Black woman say that when she showed up at her workplace she was able to do *only* the job she was hired to do. We're not only expected, we're required (voluntold) to go above and beyond what other, average, employees are able to do in order to get the same "outstanding" or even "satisfactory" box checked on our annual reviews. The expectation of fixing an organizational problem and giving 200 percent to the work often comes with the additional expectation of displaying a comforting, motherly presence while we are doing so. In the more than eighty years since Parkhurst Guzman's essay, the ways we view Black women continue to be "standardized and institutionalized by sentiment."

A dear friend of mine was the director of a small mixed-race staff. As the only Black woman in a position of power, and one of two Black women at the nonprofit, she was constantly mammified by the organization. My friend rarely fulfilled this role and, as such, was cast as the Sapphire. This led to obvious conflict within the organization and the perception that she wasn't doing her job. She had been hired to save the company from financial collapse and had excelled at the tasks in her job description. Under her leadership, the company was thriving. But her unwritten role was going unfulfilled. She wasn't leading from a place of motherly affection and wasn't coddling her employees, which left them feeling disgruntled under her leadership.

This friend and I were sitting on a bench outside a tattoo parlor, and trading stories of caucacity in the workplace over donuts. When I was a few bites in, she shared that during some recent mediation, she was told by a "neutral" third party that she needs to be "a softer place for feelings to land" for her staff.

I coughed up a few crumbs. "No they *did not!*"

"Girl, yes, they did," she replied.

"Nooooo! WTF does that even meeeean?! Where was that in your job description?!"

I was floored. Had my friend been of any other race, of any other caste, this would never, ever have happened. Of course I finished my donut, but it was with a bunch of angry bites that I did so.

It was so relatable for where I was in my life. I had returned to UC Davis, my undergraduate alma mater, as a clinical dietitian a few years prior with a two-point plan for success while working there: do the work I was getting paid to do, and leave work at work. I even interviewed stating my commitment to body politics and how

I bring it into my work so my colleagues will be prepared when I added political and historical context. I was planning to work there for at least twenty years. Great job, great people, benefits, and a pension; what could go wrong?

Having been open about what I bring to my work, I felt comfortable giving feedback about the eating disorder care UC Davis was providing. I had heard specific concerns from colleagues outside my department about the body image curriculum in use. I was familiar with the Body Project from my first job in college health and knew that it centered thin, able-bodied, white, cis, young women.[*] I attempted to address concerns about the curriculum with my colleagues casually but was met with initial resistance to look critically at the project. I asked for a meeting with a few of the therapists at the counseling center on campus and a couple other dietitians to discuss the messages we were sending to students about their bodies.

In the end, I recommended that the department end the use of the curriculum and seek out something that centered students who are invisible to the eating disorder elites and are most impacted by the body stories written by white supremacy. It was an awkward and ultimately unproductive meeting. There were Big Feelings from white therapists defending its use and desiring to salvage what we could. It has worked for some; therefore, it's good enough for all.

---

[*] Part of NEDA (the National Eating Disorders Association, the largest nonprofit organization dedicated to supporting individuals and families affected by eating disorders), the Body Project "is a group-based intervention that provides a forum for high school girls and college aged women to confront unrealistic appearance ideals and develop healthy body image and self-esteem. It has repeatedly been shown to effectively reduce body dissatisfaction, negative mood, unhealthy dieting and disordered eating." This program is a prevention program ("The Body Project," National Eating Disorders Association, https://www.nationaleatingdisorders.org/get-involved/the-body-project).

At the end of that day, I was packing up my belongings when a last-minute instant message came through on our internal Web system. It was one of the therapists from the meeting; I'll call her Melanie. She was following up that evening to tell me that she was, actually, Brown. In a lengthy message, Melanie told me that I could count on her to share her experiences about being a woman of color, that I wasn't alone; we now had something in common that I hadn't known about two minutes prior. We were on the same team. I responded with a simple "thanks for letting me know," logged off, and left the office to catch the 5:10 bus. I didn't think much about it the rest of the evening, since it wasn't anything I hadn't heard before.

Many times over the years I have been the vessel into which colleagues and clinicians choose to pour their newfound understanding of privilege. I've also been expected, multiple times, in multiple work environments, to nurture colleagues in the dominant caste after they share that, instead of the whiteness society has assigned them, they identify as Brown. Said disclosures are nothing new to me and my Black friends. I typically do not engage with these reveals and hope to sneak out of the conversation unscathed. I try to exit without the implied expectation that the colleague and I now have the same lived experiences.

After the instant message disclosure, I returned to my office the next morning and I found a meeting on my calendar that hadn't been there the evening before. I knew what it was about. At ten a.m., Melanie's supervisor, who I will call Kathy, came in my office, perched on my brown suede couch in front of my black-and-white floral wallpaper. I crossed my legs—right over the left—and took a deep breath. I clasped my hands in my lap and waited for what I knew was about to happen: the talking-to. Mind you, Kathy was on my hiring committee when I laid out everything that I'm about and would bring to this work. She had told me that the org needed diverse perspectives. Yet here she was, in my office, about to tell me that those perspectives are only valuable in theory, that they don't actually work in application.

According to Kathy, Melanie had received my brief reply and "burst into tears." She had gone right to Kathy for support. Apparently, I'd done something wrong?

Kathy told me that I was supposed to have said something powerful. I was supposed to have made Melanie feel seen. I was told that Melanie is doing Hard Work in unpacking her racial identity, and I should have been there for her.

Girl, what? Me?!

Unbeknownst to me, I had been expected to be a natural nurturer for Melanie. I was told I was supposed to have celebrated her disclosure and offered to shepherd her in her development. It was my role to make her feel seen.

I should have been a soft place for her feelings to land.

But I wasn't.

I was fidgeting in my chair by now, slightly swiveling right and left. Kathy asked that I follow up with Melanie, that I ask her to lunch, offer support, and build a bond over a shared experience. Not only would it be helpful to Melanie, it was in the best interest of the eating disorder management team that I repair this. I needed to clean up this mess.

I had hung a smaller print of *Breathe Beauty* in this university office. I looked at the figure, hoping to see something, anything, that would get me through this conversation. Sighing, I asked Kathy if she had talked about passing privilege with Melanie or the caste dynamics at play. I had never been assigned whiteness and there was a privilege differential that I would need to tiptoe around if Melanie and I were to talk about how I came (was born) into my racial identity and align my experience with hers. Kathy had not discussed or thought about this.

Now, nowhere in my job duties was there a line about colleague racial identity development and support; I didn't remember anything in the interview asking me about my ability to nurture and coddle feelings. No one told me I would be asked to spend the money I earned there to pay for awkward lunches. I was caught off guard, but I wasn't surprised. This was definitely chipping away at my two-point plan.

I declined Kathy's suggestion that I ask Melanie to lunch and in so doing disrupted the expectations of me as Mammy, a role they had subconsciously hired me to fill. Kathy used this opportunity to tell me that I needed to stop questioning the status quo of the department's eating disorder care and body image curriculum; the clinicians were using "best practices" for treating clients with eating disorders, and I need not bring up my concerns about anti-fatness or anti-Blackness anymore. Another eating disorder therapist had a personal connection to the curriculum and was feeling "attacked" by campus colleagues who had shared their concerns about the program with me. All of this was damaging the team. I was then labeled as "difficult to communicate with." I was cast as the Sapphire, the Angry Black Woman. It became clear that if I wasn't going to fulfill my role as Mammy, I was only to be seen and not heard going forward. And that was that.

When Kathy left, I glanced at *Breathe Beauty* once more; there was nothing that could have prevented that interrogation, but the painting did bring me comfort. My gaze then shifted to a photo of my mentee, Lexi, and my spouse. They were going to hear yet another story of me failing to meet a white woman's expectations of coddling and comfort. And they would likely have the same response: it's not going to get better, it's time to think about leaving.

I've heard similar stories from many Black friends and colleagues. Many of us don't even recognize the absurdity and anti-Blackness in the moment. And often, just to survive, we gaslight ourselves and pretend it never happened.

There is not a playbook for Black women who refuse to don Mammy's apron and red kerchief in the workplace.

Having been marked as the Sapphire at that job was a turning point. Almost all feedback I offered in the collaborations between dietitians and therapists was cast as negative. The therapists in the eating disorder area no longer took my phone calls to coordinate care, thus requiring coordination and consultation to be sent through the medical record only. The following year one of Kathy's therapist trainees shared that she avoided talking to me on the phone to coordinate care, as she felt like taking my call meant she was in trouble . . . with the Angry Black Woman.

The deterioration between departments and in client care was obvious to me but wasn't a priority for anyone else. The eating disorder therapists referred only to my colleague. She was a thin white woman who is great at her job yet was not the best fit for *every* student on campus; nor was I, which is why we had two.

Only when writing this book in the summer of 2021 did I realize how much the assignment of these narratives weighed on me.

In late July of 2021, I had an acute seizure flare, my first in five years, with multiple occurring in a short period of time. My memory wasn't holding up and I was regularly exhausted. I called my neurologist for his advice and he convinced me to take a month off from working at UC Davis to let my brain chemicals recalibrate. I hadn't realized that my job had become impossible to do while being hypervigilant, receiving inappropriate emails from Kathy, and waiting for another one-on-one ambush. I was devastated that I wasn't able to push through. If I'm honest, I was looking for someone to tell me to finally sit down. I had a long history of enduring this kind of bullshit. Apparently, I hadn't learned any lessons from my past flares. I was resentful of my body for outwardly expressing weakness when I needed to perform resilience. I was embarrassed and fearful to admit my vulnerability and to ask for the time off. I was a mess. But this time I was knocking on forty and realized this wasn't sustainable until retirement. I had kept telling myself that the caucacity of my coworkers couldn't bury me. Instead, I was doing the burying for them; I was digging an early grave.

The same morning I acquiesced to my neurologist's recommendations, Lexi phoned me just to chat. Somehow she called just as I was wrapping up a call with my boss, having shared that I would be taking the next month off for medical leave.

A couple weeks later, while still on leave, I interviewed Lexi for an episode of *My Black Body Podcast*, a limited podcast series about the intersections of Blackness, eating disorders, fatness, queerness, and generally what it's like to be a Black woman/femme in the United States. We were experiencing some echoing in the mics while recording, so we both ended up in pillow and blanket forts with our recording equipment. It was the softness I needed during that time. We recalled the day that I finally agreed that it was time to sit down and take time off. I reflected with her, "As I was hanging up that call, you were calling on the other line, and I was still mid-meltdown. [I told you] 'I'm . . . letting my coworkers down and letting my patients down. I am just an awful, awful human.' And this is also . . . mid-Olympics. Do you remember what you said to me?" I asked.

Lexi tried to remember. "What did I say? It was that, like, because Simone [Biles] had just pulled out of the team final and we were really . . . praising her for her courage and being able to take care of herself and not fall into that trap of just continually suffering for your team, for your coworkers, for your patients, and everything. I was like, 'We just talked about this. We just talked about this, Jessica. This is the same thing!' I was like, 'You are Simone.'"

Now, I am definitely not Simone Biles, but I appreciated the reflection. It made me see outside of myself and acknowledge the bigger pattern. Biles embodied resilience and perseverance. She never showed weakness, always pushed through. I had wailed into the phone with despair and giant tears splattered onto the table the morning Lexi made this connection, and she thought she'd said something wrong. Instead, she'd held up the mirror I'd refused to face; I didn't have to do this, I could say no.

Into 2022, amid a new batch of eating disorder therapist trainees, Kathy hadn't let things go. She was persistently trying to get me to meet with her one-on-one (nope), and during a meeting with me, my colleagues, and my boss she shared that I was to blame, entirely, for her eating disorder trainees' poor experience at UC Davis. It had been a big problem for her and she needed me to be integrated into the next round of hiring so that everyone could have a better time (read: act appropriately and follow unwritten rules).

I clarified, "Kathy, you think *I* was to blame for your trainees' lack of clinical development?!"

"Well, yes, whatever happened with the Body Project and your feedback about the program set the tone for the trainees for the past three years and—"

"Well, Kathy," I interrupted, "I'm happy to report that your problem, *me*, has been solved. I've already given notice; my last day is in two weeks."

I finally said no.

• • •

THE MOMENT BILES DECIDED TO PULL HERSELF OUT OF competition at the Tokyo Olympics, she was labeled a quitter. She was mocked on social media and told she was selfish and had let her country down.[12] "I've done gymnastics on broken ribs. My two broken big toes are shattered (because they're not just broken, they're shattered, in pieces), kidney stones. I've been through sexual abuse. I came back to the sport. There are so many barriers that I've gotten past. And so to say, I just had a bad turn and quit. If you look at all of those, you could see I'm not a quitter. I'm a fighter." Biles vlogged about her Olympic experience for the Facebook series *Simone vs Herself*, and this is what she said after she pulled herself out of the gymnastics competition after getting the twisties and not feeling like she could compete safely. "We're not cats, we don't have nine lives and I just felt like a flying rag doll."[13]

During the podcast episode I recorded with Lexi, a former gymnast herself, I asked her what it meant to watch Biles pull out of the Olympics gymnastics lineup. "It was just so amazing to be able to see her actually say, like, 'No, I need to take care of myself,'" Lexi replied. "'This is dangerous. This is not worth it. These people with these stars and stripes painted across their faces can take a walk if all they care about is a gold medal, and they don't actually care about my safety,' which is something super new to see in the Olympic cycle. It's always been about 'compete on your broken ankle because we want the gold for gymnastics.' . . . So the fact that she took a stand against that was like a revolutionary moment, honestly."

"Did you notice it impacting you or the people around you and how you were talking about either gymnastics or mental health or anything like that?" I asked.

"Absolutely," she answered. "I think that it impacted me because I felt the same way in regards to putting all else above gymnastics, no matter what. Like, putting your mental health aside, putting everything aside to get the gold, and the fact that she was able to break that cycle and break that mold felt like I was able to breathe a little bit easier, and it allowed a lot of people, I think, in this Olympic cycle and kind of like in everyone's daily lives to be, like, 'What am I doing?'"

She continued, "And we saw that in Naomi Osaka, and we saw that in a couple of tennis players, and I think divers, as well, that pulled out of the Olympics cycle while they were in Tokyo because of mental health issues. And to be able to see someone at their prime and in the biggest moment of their life having the courage to do that, it gives, I think, everyone else a little bit of a boost in courageousness in their everyday lives to put themselves first."

Biles has since talked about her choice to persevere: "If you looked at everything I've gone through for the past seven years, I should have never made another Olympic team," she told *The Cut*. "I should have quit way before Tokyo, when Larry Nassar was in the media for two years. It was too much. But I was not going to let him take something I've worked for since I was six years old. I wasn't going to let him take that joy away from me. So I pushed past that for as long as my mind and my body would let me."[14]

She was resilient. And having prioritized herself at the Olympics, it didn't kill her. Simone Biles had the last word on the subject when she wrote on Instagram, "I've pushed through so much the past couple years, the word *quitter* is not in my vocabulary. for some of you that may be how you define me but keep talking because I can't hear you over my 7 olympic medals which tied me for the most decorated gymnast EVER as well as the most decorated american gymnast."[15]

• • •

KETANJI BROWN JACKSON WAS ALSO ABLE TO HAVE THE LAST word. After sitting through days of absurd questioning and, frankly, harassment from elected officials, she was confirmed as a Supreme Court justice by the US Senate on April 7, 2022. Almost two years after the 2020 protests, Judge Brown Jackson had been grilled by senators, and her body was a battlefield over which they participated in political theater and signaled their allegiance to their constituents.

Her nomination was the result of a pledge presidential candidate Joe Biden made in February 2020 to put a Black woman on the Supreme Court should he be given the opportunity.[16] It turns out that this was one promise he could make to Black voters and actually keep. Biden was the most lackluster Democratic presidential candidate many of the voting public had seen in their lifetimes. Even before much of white America jumped on the Black Girl Magic train, Biden was banking on the symbolism of a Black woman to energize his campaign.

There is a problem with a train, though. It makes stops along the way and eventually when it reaches its final destination everyone departs, which is exactly what happened for Black folks by 2021. A year after the protests following the death of George Floyd, support for Black Lives Matter was *lower* among white people than it had been in the beginning of 2020.[17] Along with all other racial groups, white folks had had a sharp increase in support for BLM in 2020, but it wasn't sustained. Additionally, one year later, only $250 million had been spent or committed to a specific initiative after US companies pledged $50 billion during racial justice protests.[18] Virtue signaling and performative allyship at its finest. It turned out the "listening," "learning," and commitments to business culture and societal change were excellent branding but lacked all accountability.

The racial reckoning wasn't. And Black women continue to be relied upon to solve problems centuries in the making, to be the special aliens.

• • •

BLACK WOMEN ARE OFTEN NOT AFFORDED COMPLEXITY AND THE capacity to be more than one thing. We're good for our labor, and when we don't comply with expectations, we're discarded.

I love being Black, and some days, I'd sure love to quit fighting to be seen as something other than a Sapphire or a Mammy or a Special Alien and just be average; at least one time each day I pine for the ability to be basic.

I want to be Basic Black.

I want to look at the bell curve and see myself and my work square in the middle, perhaps right at the top of the hump, a solid average individual. I bet the view is amazing from on high, and the grass is greener up there because they actually have the time to water it. I want to be one of those 68 percent of people around the center point of the curve who are asked how they're doing and mean it when they respond "Fine."

A B-minus type of average on the report card that receives an "as long as you tried your hardest" response is what I want to aim for. I want to proudly display the participation ribbon I was "awarded" at the science fair. I want to be the average employee who is late to work every day because, "Gosh, the line at Starbucks was around the block this morning!" I want my productivity level to imply that I enjoy my job, but I have things to do in my life that are more important than my output. I want to have the space, time, and resources to invest in these interests, which would include things like drinking rosé all day and thrift store shopping for wooden furniture that I will refinish just to make it look old.

Everyone is familiar with the line "God, give me the confidence of a mediocre white dude." I want to try on mediocrity. I bet it feels like a weighted blanket. I want to just *be*.

chapter three

"For Our Own Good": Respectability

I N THE PROCESS OF WRITING THIS BOOK I LEARNED THAT MANY Black folks in my personal and professional lives hadn't heard the word *respectability* before. I found myself struggling to define it, but could come up with examples to which people could relate. How the Obamas needed to act while in the White House worked, as did discussing the comedian Mo'Nique's message to her Instagram followers on May 29, 2021. Eleven years after thanking Hattie Mc-Daniel for enduring, she decided to go on Instagram Live from a hotel room in Jackson, Mississippi. Wearing only a gray bathrobe and with her hair in gray braids, she started talking to her audience. She had a message for her followers, particularly young Black women who call her Auntie: stop leaving the house wearing your bonnets, head scarves, pajamas, and slippers. Period.

She had questions.

The question that I'm having to your sweet babies: when did we
lose pride in representing ourselves? When did we step away of:
let me make sure I'm presentable when I leave my home; lemme
make sure I'm representing the family I created, so if I'm out in
the street I look like I have pride?[1]

She assured us that this plea was coming from a place of love. "It
took me a minute to say what I'm g[etting] read' to say, cuz I want
to make sure I'm not sayin' it in judgment."

She seemed dismayed that she needed to deliver this address. She
had been excited to travel to Jackson for performances at Chuckles
Comedy House, but the sight of Black women in the airport who
were wearing clothing she felt was designated for the house and
never for the street had really dampened her spirit.

In her dissertation, she made a clear distinction between Black
women who are Queens (those who know how to dress when leaving the house) and those in Queen Training (those in scarves and
leggings in the airport). Those in the latter category need to learn
to "represent you like you are worthy, like you deserve the title of
Queen."

Not only did Mo'Nique seem to feel like she was providing an
opportunity for young Black women to step into themselves, but
she also spoke to us as if it was a Black community concern for
us all. She advised those of us worthy of the title of Queen, her
"wiser sisters," that if we see a young Black woman not living up
to her standards of Queendom, we should tap her on the shoulder
and let her know: "Baby girl, you deserve more than what you're

showing," and that by doing so we are "helping our community." She was doing us all a favor by teaching us how to act and sharing how we can uplift the race.

Mo'Nique's overall concern was clear, but she spelled it out for us at the end: "Cuz if you look like you don't give a damn, how you gon' be treated?"

But the rest of her sentence was missing: "Cuz if you look like you don't give a damn, how you gon' be treated" . . . *by white people and those invested in white supremacy?*

Mentioning this video or its synopsis to Black folks created an instant understanding of what respectability looks like. Some were taken aback that there was a word for something they'd grown up their whole lives not examining. The idea that these conversations were directly tied to whiteness elicited both surprise and some relief that what they had experienced was, indeed, not okay and had deeper roots beyond their own family.

• • •

AT THE BEGINNING OF THE COVID-19 PANDEMIC, I, LIKE MANY others, quickly transitioned to remote work. All of a sudden, I had two sets of sweatpants in rotation: work sweats and sleep sweats. I was among the many to realize that zippers and bras were severely overrated. It was the first time I could say that I leaned into athleisure; I was loving my basic wardrobe. When my spouse wanted to invest in some basictivity herself and purchase equipment for a New York–based online exercise class platform, I didn't object. I felt like it would go right alongside the lifestyle I was aiming to achieve. The platform has a very Positive Vibes Only feel, with opportunities to find other users with similar interests using hashtags like #BeersAfter, #FeelGoodLookGood, and of course we need #SweatingForTheWedding.

In early fall 2020, I was sing-sweating my way through a class, as the instructor was going through the list of people who had met a milestone during the ride. She gave a shout-out to a member whose username was @NotThatKaren (I said it was a basic platform). The instructor followed up by halting her movement, standing up, and opening her arms wide to give "a shout-out to all of the Karens out there! I feel like y'all have been having a hard year and you don't deserve that!"

Really.

Again, this is a New York City–based company. To recap, earlier that year, Amy Cooper, a white woman, called the cops on Christian Cooper (no relation), a Black man and bird-watcher.[*] Mr. Cooper was bird-watching in Central Park and had asked Ms. Cooper to put her cocker spaniel on a leash so it didn't continue to disrupt the birds' habitat, in accordance with park rules. Not only did Ms. Cooper reject the preposterous idea that the rules actually applied to her, but she also decided to challenge every other Karen for peak Karenship and called 911 to report that Mr. Cooper was assaulting her.

Now, we know that white womanhood and its virtue are important in the United States, and over the centuries we've seen to what lengths people, particularly white men, will go to protect them. But the Karens up the ante on white womanhood. "The white women we're talking about are positioning themselves as the victims of some sort of offense and they're in need of institutional protec-

---

[*] Christian Cooper will star in a National Geographic TV show, *Extraordinary Birder*.

tion," Gene Demby put it during the "What's in a 'Karen'" episode of the NPR podcast *Code Switch*.[2] And this is what makes Karening unique: white women's reliance on institutional entities like the police to protect them.

While wailing into the phone at her 911 operator, Amy Cooper chose not to report that someone had simply asked her to put her dog on a leash and she just wanted to pout about it, oh no. She chose to weaponize her whiteness, to yell that a Black man was assaulting her and she needed to be rescued. This Black man had made her feel like she was a victim and now he was going to experience the consequences leveled by the institutions built to protect whiteness.

I was downright confused when the Karens got the energetic, enthusiastic, and specific support on the exercise platform. One week after this Central Park incident, and following the murder of George Floyd, this company had announced their commitment to anti-racism. This company even held some exercise classes dedicated to emotional healing and activism, broadly speaking. The company was signaling to us that it was paying attention.

The company's commitment to anti-racism via social media was good timing and good branding; getting on board with the BLM bandwagon was a must for any corporation's 2020 bingo card. This company told us it was different from the others, but where was the follow-through only months later? With the memory of Ms. Cooper tugging on her dog's leash hard enough to lift the spaniel off the ground while screaming at Christian Cooper, along with recollections of Permit Patty, BBQ Becky, and another New York nightmare, Cornerstone Caroline, I sent a message with a couple queries to four of the exercise company's generic *contact us* email addresses provided.

A week later I'd heard nothing. In the interim, I shared this with some folks who were similarly confused about both the situation and why I hadn't even gotten a generic form letter reply.

The performance of companies virtue signaling when it's trendy only to go back to business as usual was tired. Was this going to be a member of the cohort of corporations that had pledged $50 billion for "racial justice" yet had barely spent anything a year later?[3] I was curious.

And I had time.

I asked the internet for their thoughts. After doing so, I received a four-paragraph reply from the company's "support" email account assuring me that there was no ill intent and that the company "believe[s] in inclusion, love, acceptance and support and stand[s] firmly behind those values." They assured me that the shout-out in question "was meant to be a lighthearted moment" and that I had "misinterpreted" the entire situation because it was only about people named Karen.

I'd already seen for myself how inclusive the platform was. Folks connecting with #BlackLivesMatter were stacked along people screaming that #POLICELIVESMATTER [sic]. To this day people connecting with #CelebrateBlackJoy are alongside those who are ready for #Trump2024. The company really is about acceptance. I must not have understood.

"Inclusion, Love, Acceptance" reads like a bumper sticker on a Prius or a quote on a rainbow sticker available in June. I clearly should have lived, laughed, and loved at the lighthearted moment. I was the problem.

After this non-apology, someone on the internet shared an article about a class on the platform that had recently been removed because the instructor said something to the effect of not caring that there was COVID in the White House, as long as it wasn't in the NFL.[4] A professor in Texas shared her outrage about this statement in a Facebook group. The company was bringing politics into exercise and she wasn't here for it. The CEO of the company responded and apologized swiftly and directly. "You're right. We're better than this. We're taking it down." And Just Like That, it was gone.

Are you curious? There was a stark discrepancy in prioritization of both member demographics and political values here. I sent another email asking about this and I got a response from a Black executive at the company who was willing to chat later that week. By then, I had the original questions and many more. I agreed to the call, curious to hear more about her work and her thoughts.

• • •

THE CALL WAS WILD. THE EXEC WAS A DARK-SKINNED, THIN Black woman with long straight hair. From the waist up, she was dressed in what I took to be what a True Professional in New York would wear, while I was wearing my most competent-looking cozy sweater. I had the "touch up my appearance" function on Zoom turned all the way up for this meeting to give the illusion I'd put on makeup for the occasion.

We began what was supposed to be a thirty-minute listening (to me) session that turned into a forty-five-minute talking (at me) session. She even asked her assistant to move her next meeting so "we" could keep talking. The narrative was predictable, I smiled slightly, nodded politely, and worked very hard to keep my eyebrows in check until the speech was over. The vibe was close to the one Mo'Nique provided during her video about bonnets. The exec seemed to be speaking her truth with composure, coming only from a place of love, just as Mo'Nique had done.

The conversation included some of what I think are keys to enforcing the narratives for how Black people, especially Black women, need to behave in society.

ESTABLISH AUTHORITY AND BUILD A RELATIONSHIP

Make sure that the other Black woman knows that you speak for the experience of all Black women and that you can be trusted to know about which you speak.

To start us off, the executive shared that, even though she is an African immigrant, I need not worry, she knows all about the experience of Black American women. She assured me that she may have married a white man, but they have a young daughter whose skin is darker than mine, so she knows what it's like for me. She was letting me know that she *gets it*. She is not only relatable but also a credible source for how Black women should behave in the United States. Noted. She let me know that because she is Black, she shares any concerns I may have about companies performing allyship. We're in alignment. I could trust her to understand the experiences and concerns of all Black women. She assured me that this company is the Real Thing. It has a true, ongoing commitment to anti-racism work.

PRIORITIZE WHITENESS AND WHITE FEELINGS AND GASLIGHT THE EXPERIENCES OF BLACK PEOPLE

It's not a good look to question whiteness; it's how it works in this country, and we need to be respectful of this hierarchy. We need to know our place.

Despite what I thought, I was informed that this was, actually, a lighthearted moment during this ride. Ha . . . ha? It really didn't mean anything to anyone but me. Any questions I had about the company's dedication to living its commitments were unwarranted. It was just about people named Karen and had no connection to white women who use the police to enforce the social hierarchies. Case closed.

And as for the instructor, well, she is the victim here. I was told that her feelings matter and I should think about this before opening my mouth. The exec also shared that the instructor knows all about diversity because she is a member of the LGBTQ community (ummm . . . same), and because of this she couldn't ever say anything racist.

It was clear whose experiences were important. The instructor's and the woman who was upset about the mention of COVID in the White House. Mine? Not so much.

ENFORCE THE IDEA THAT ONE'S INDIVIDUAL ACTIONS REFLECT ON BLACK WOMEN AS A MONOLITH

Don't bring down the race by making a scene and questioning whiteness. Invest in impression management.

When a Black woman draws public attention for questioning whiteness, she becomes a *problem* in need of proper containment. This was me. I'm the one who needs to Do Better here, I'm giving all Black folks a bad name. She was telling me this for my own good, and going forward, hopefully I will learn to be quiet. I should be grateful for this lesson.

DISTRACT FROM THE CORE ISSUE AND ORIGINAL CONCERN

The initial concern doesn't even matter in the end.

The exec and I never got around to discussing the social structures and stratifications that had brought us to that moment, and
the dynamic that had been set up between the two of us as the
handler and the handled. We never talked about white supremacy,
tokenism, the narratives written about white women's frailty, or the
expectations for Black women to both act in accordance with and
enforce respectability.

It was a hot mess. I felt outside of myself, watching it unfold.
I could see the part of me that was laughing and giving all of the
raised eyebrows, but the outward-facing Jessica kept it together.

It went unsaid that the separation between us was engineered.
What happened was by design; it unfolded in the way it was supposed to. The executive was incredibly skillful. She did an excellent
job at handling the situation, at handling me.

To be clear, I harbor no ill will to this executive, none whatso-
ever. I get it. I will never blame a Black woman for successfully navigating white supremacy. If I'd wanted to climb a corporate ladder,
I could have even learned something from her. (No thank you.) I
understand the desire to have closer proximity to whiteness.

I finally got to talk as we were wrapping up. She asked me if
there was anything that I would like to discuss, and after sitting
through the last forty minutes I promptly inquired when they
were going to get some size diversity on their platform. She told
me, "Well, that's a tough one because this is the *fitness* industry."
I choked on my pamplemousse LaCroix and almost dropped the
can. We were done.

• • •

MY FRIENDS AND I HAVE NOT BEEN ABLE TO PINPOINT EXACTLY when we learned about respectability. I remember introducing the concept of palatability to my dad. "Obama has to be the white man's Black man." He got it, and shared that he felt similarly about some of the most respected civil rights leaders "back in my day." He told me stories of those he thought sold out for a watered-down message that could be more acceptable.

The idea of respectability in the Black community was born in the late nineteenth century from the Black elite. Pitcan and co-authors in their article "Performing a Vanilla Self: Respectability Politics, Social Class, and the Digital World" provide this definition: "'Respectability politics' describes a self-presentation strategy historically adopted by African-American women to reject White stereotypes by promoting morality while de-emphasizing sexuality" and "subordinated groups frequently use these tactics to gain upward mobility."

They describe respectability politics as having three main factors:

1. "It reinforces within-group stratification to juxtapose a respectable against a shameful other."
2. "Respectability endorses values that contradict stereotypes, such as presenting Black women as modest, thereby enforcing a dominant narrative that women should exercise sexual restraint."
3. "Practicing respectability involves impression management to align with White, middle-class indicators of class status and privilege, such as using standard English rather than African American Vernacular English in racially mixed audiences."[5]

The use of the term *audiences* in number three seems as intentional as it is curious. It invokes the idea that there is a select group of individuals watching and listening as Black folks just try to live our lives. It brings forth the necessity of performance. Black women know this reality well. We know when we're being readily observed in mixed company, when we've felt surveilled in what should have been a neutral environment.

Paisley Jane Harris notes that Black women were more vulnerable to the politics of respectability than were men in the nineteenth century. Black women were more likely to both use them and be judged by them. "Moreover, African American women symbolized, even embodied, this concept."[6] Consistent with what we've seen, the burden of white supremacy disproportionately impacts Black women.

Behaving and dressing in accordance with respectability provides both safety and structure. It creates clear distinctions between in- and out-groups. For those looking to increase their social capital, it assists with choosing those to befriend and those to avoid. It provides specific ways of being that are clear enough to obey in order to hopefully mitigate any additional harm from whiteness.

A friend of mine looked to these ways as "guardrails" while she was growing up. Her appearance was policed by her father, who had strict ideas for how she should dress and what made an acceptable hairstyle; ponytails needed to lie completely flat. The idea that there was a system in place to keep her on track made it safer for her to exist in a society that is invested in her erasure. It makes sense. Living in the United States can seem like a navigation of landmines. This friend loves Stacey Abrams, who provides a vision and specific ways to be involved in activism, a clear path. Abrams provides my friend with a clear structure, which makes it safer to be involved in politics. Abrams, in my experience and from what I could find, is rarely described as angry, and definitely not as a Jezebel. She has found a way to navigate her Blackness in a way that maintains palatability.

This same friend and I talk about my message and how it's a particular audience that will resonate with me. I ask folks to sit with the discomfort of not having an immediate solution to a societal problem and of having hard and awkward conversations about the narratives we've been told about our bodies. My passion and conviction can be interpreted as anger. I am not one to make myself small in order to get a seat at the table. You could say that I'm not the respectable type.

* * *

WHAT MAY BE THE INTENTIONS OF BLACK WOMEN TO PROTECT each other from the harm of whiteness misses the mark when we reinforce a right and wrong way to be. We reinforce this harm by policing the appearance and actions of our sisters around us. We shame those who don't conform. Rather than having white people be the ones to discipline our bodies, it often first comes from those who love us the most. It makes sense when Black women tell those who aren't following the rules of respectability to know that we need to be doing so. We care about each other. A lot.

In fall of 2021, I invited three of my rad fat Black friends and professional crushes to a Zoom gathering to share their experiences with respectability. Shana (she/her), Fresh (she/they, fluidly), Ifasina (they/them), and I hadn't all been in the same place at the same time since we were in Oakland for the 2015 NOLOSE conference.

NOLOSE, "a diverse, vibrant community of fat queer and trans folks and our allies, with a shared commitment to intersectional anti-oppression ideology and action, seeking to end the oppression of fat people!"[7] kicked off the conference with the BIPOC-only day. Shana and I connected because we were two of the three-person team that had been asked to plan that day's events. I met Fresh at the conference, and she became a professional crush after I heard about their work as a community-based edible activist, chef, and farmer in Chicago. Ifasina and I had met through fat activist and body liberation spaces, and I got lucky enough to share office space with them as they did Reiki and coaching work in Oakland. The first half of the call was catching up, recalling memories, and setting intentions to be in the same place at the same time once the pandemic ended. When I steered the conversation to respectability Ifasina was not surprised when I shared that I'd talked to some Black folks who hadn't been introduced to the concept. "For them it's just another Tuesday," they said.

Shana shared an experience from her late twenties. "I was out at a bar with a mixed group of friends, but mostly not Black people . . . when I stepped away to use the restroom and came back, this fat Black woman stopped me on my way back to tell me 'You're being too loud. You're making a scene. You're embarrassing yourself. You're embarrassing all of us.' And I don't remember. She just went on, and I was not happy. She was older than me, of course, and clearly came from a place of, like, concern, [thinking] 'I got to intervene. This is not how we act in public.'"

The older woman was aware of the audience; she knew whiteness was watching and it was her role to align with what this situation demanded from her, which included making sure that Shana did the same.

Centuries of demonizing messages take their toll. Black women can't escape this culture's belief that Black women's bodies are inherently "too much" and this can result in shame about ourselves and our bodies. According to psychologists John A. Terrizzi Jr. and Natalie Shook, shame functions to maintain social hierarchies. Consequently, Black women's body shame is not only harmful for the individual but also serves as a tool to uphold white supremacy. Shana noted this in her experience with the older Black woman at the bar: "She was probably uncomfortable in that space, too. Sitting in the restaurant, [the woman and her date] were probably the only Black people there and uncomfortable in her skin. She was wearing one of those, like, all black, drapey outfits that you wear when you're not feeling comfortable in your body." Wearing outfits that hide our bodies in situations where we're already hypervisible can be one way we attempt to guard ourselves against being too much, all while knowing it is impossible to do so.

Shana said of her interaction at the bar, "So I was heated, and so I left her. I went back over to the bar and my friends were like, 'What happened?' and I said, 'I don't want to talk about it.' And finally, one of my white friends just pestered me, and so I explained what had happened. And it felt like a betrayal of this Black woman to tell this white friend what had happened. And I felt like I was so angry at [the other Black woman] that to reject that attempt to police my behavior was then to reject her. And it felt . . . like a betrayal of her. Totally misguided and ridiculous, but still coming from a place of, like, care and control."

Ifasina agreed. "I think that this is the thing about respectability that doesn't get talked about. We often only talk about that we understand where it comes from because Black folks had to do what they had to do to survive slavery, to survive Jim Crow, to survive capitalism, like, I get it. But there's this way that we turn it in on each other that then creates rejection and disconnection from each other."

Shana shared that "it made me think about . . . when I have to reject someone else's use of respectability placed on me, it means that I have to reject their Blackness." All four of us on the call could relate to the distance created when another Black person tells us how to perform for whiteness. From family members who may have been "well intentioned" to colleagues who think they are mentoring us when they show us how not to behave. We'd all been in relationships in which a fissure had developed after someone attempted to locate the problem on us rather than on whiteness.

● ● ●

ONE SUMMER MORNING, MY POPS AND I WERE STANDING ON MY front porch and I asked if I could show him Mo'Nique's video about what Black women should not wear outside. He was born in rural Georgia in the 1940s, and I wondered if he would resonate with Mo'Nique's thesis. We sat down on the stoop together, he straightened his short-bill cap, and I pulled my phone out of my back pocket and cued up the video. He watched the first five or ten seconds of the video. He sighed, then stopped watching and stared off into the direction of my vegetable garden as the video continued to play. It was unclear whether he was listening to Mo'Nique or critiquing my farming attempts. The video finished and I waited for his response. "What'd you think, Dad?" I asked. He was quiet and contemplative; I get my practicality from him. After a long pause, his initial statement was simple: "Well, she didn't like it," referring to seeing bonnets in the airport.

Indeed.

With some additional probing for his observations, he tied his experience growing up to what Mo'Nique was participating in. He recalled how a friend of his, who I'll call Shirley, would respond when seeing a Black woman on the street who didn't meet her expectations for how Black women should dress and present ourselves. Shirley took it personally when Black women wore clothing she felt didn't show pride around white folks. She thought it reflected poorly on all Black women when one of us dyed our hair blond or wore a blond wig, something reserved for white people. "It's so embarrassing to us," Shirley would say. She seemed to have the same concerns about the Black community as Mo'Nique, though Shirley's comments were in the 1950s and 1960s and Mo'Nique's came sixty years later.

My dad didn't understand why the two Black women cared so much about how other Black women dressed and behaved. "It ain't affecting you." Which, in the exact moment, may be true, but in the larger context might not be. Mo'Nique knows this and my dad's friend knows it, too. That my dad didn't know this was consistent with the gender disparities in the policing of bodies and also with his IDGAF philosophies for living life.

I was curious whether others in the family received these messages, so I texted my dad's older sister to see if she would like to join the conversation. I set up what turned out to be my dad's first Zoom call, fifteen months into the pandemic. My aunt's mic and camera weren't always in alignment, something blamed on my cousins, but we figured out how to connect. I played Mo'Nique's video from my phone so my aunt could listen. When it was over I asked her and my dad to tell me about their collective responses.

My aunt was cool, calm, and collected in her response. She did not agree with Mo'Nique's use of profanity, but didn't disagree with the sentiment. When an elder decides to approach someone with concerns about their appearance, she believes it's best to build a relationship first, and be respectful, to not use four-letter words. My aunt thinks it is important to encourage appropriate attire and behavior. She shared her personal story of building a relationship with a young man who walked along her street before she told him to pull up his pants as he walks around town. My aunt agreed with the comedian that women need to take pride in their appearance in order to signal to others that "I am a woman of worth." Specifically, she believes this does not include clothing items like dresses with slits up to their rear end. She believes it's important to "dress for the occasion," to which my dad agreed.

My father shared that he views the way that many Black folks dress today as a form of protest. My aunt agreed, though she believes our clothing decisions should not be offensive to anyone else. Specifically, women's breasts and men's rear ends and underwear do not need to be on display. Her sentiments were consistent with the idea that Black women have a responsibility to be modest when out in public lest they be subject to the stereotype of the hypersexualized Jezebel.

We shared our love and goodbyes and ended the call. I put my elbow on the dining room table and rested my chin on my hand as

I continued to think through their comments. My aunt seemed to align with Mo'Nique's message and was consistent with the playbook used by the exercise executive: build a relationship and establish authority. I hadn't gone into the call with any clear expectations, but I was still surprised by what I heard. It brought home the ways that respectability has been employed and reinforced in my family among my aunts, uncle, and cousins. Things were rough for my dad and his siblings growing up, and I saw how performing respectability could shield them from some of the chaos. How playing by the rules might maintain social standing. I continued to put these pieces together, something I hadn't thought to do before writing this book. I saw how our family connections might have developed if whiteness hadn't gotten in the way.

I turned to my left and asked my dad to expand on his thoughts about clothing as protest. He told me that he and his siblings had to dress up as kids when leaving the house because you couldn't look "too niggerish." This is where his thoughts about "dressing for the occasion" originate. He told me that participating in the respectability politics of his youth didn't work for their generation; "white folks continued to disrespect Black folks" despite their refined dress. He believes that the younger generations saw this discrepancy and figured "Why should I dress to impress white society if white society isn't going to care about the lives and well-being of Black folks?" He felt like "It didn't work, things didn't improve," so young people rebelled.

I told my dad I was grateful that he shared his thorough critique with me. And then we were able to get back to his thorough critique of my gardening attempts. Thanks, Dad.

chapter four

Too Much, Yet Not Enough: Restriction

I FIRST SAW LEXI BROWN COMPETE IN JANUARY OF 2017.

"So there's a Black gymnast who will be kneeling during the
national anthem at the first gymnastics home meet of the season
tonight." I took a sharp inhale when I read the text. I hadn't planned
on staying at work past five p.m. on a Friday, but this was reason
enough to do so. I replied to my spouse, the interim athletic trainer
for the UC Davis gymnastics team, letting her know that I'd be
there. I made a quick call to my dad to see if he could take care of
our dog for the night and set out to find something for dinner.

Forty days into my two-point plan for how to survive in the
workplace by not getting emotionally involved shriveled up and
blew away. That night I would be returning to the last building on

the UC Davis campus in which I'd been over eleven years ago. I'd graduated in that arena with my undergraduate degree in clinical nutrition, the only Black person in my class. Of course.

That day, in 2017, instead of walking in wearing regalia, I was returning in office clothes, a True Professional and product of that university. I paid for a ticket and stepped inside. It smelled the same, faintly like plastic mats, floor varnish, and all of the sports medicine topical treatments from the athletic training room on my left. I walked up the stairs and looked out over the railing at the floor below. Flo Rida's "My House" was playing on the sound system, a staple of home games. The teams were warming up on vault, uneven bars, beam, and floor, and it wasn't hard to pick out the gymnast who was going to kneel that night. Lexi was the only Black gymnast on the UC Davis gymnastics team. Of course.

Her hair was long, straight, and pulled into a messy bun like the rest of the team's. They were wearing blue and white leotards with sparkly silver swirls. She was similar in height to the other gymnasts, with broader shoulders and more muscular arms and legs than her teammates. Her wrists were taped.

The meet began and I made my way to a blue plastic bench at the north end of the arena. After reading the names of the opposing team the announcer read the names of the UC Davis gymnasts. As they were announced, each took a step forward and waved at the crowd. I learned her name: Alexis Brown. After all competitors were announced, the team held hands and remained standing for the national anthem. Lexi took a knee and bowed her head.

The crowd was asked to stand. I did not.

When holding one's breath for the entirety of the national anthem one realizes how long the song is . . . it's long. I spent it staring both at Lexi and around the room, waiting for someone to have the gall to heckle or boo so that I could take off my earrings and do something about it. Nothing happened. A few of her teammates were noticeably uncomfortable, but everyone kept it together. Things seemed to be fine. The meet began.

Lexi sprinted eighty-three feet down a narrow runway, launched herself off a springboard, and vaulted over a table, twice. After a safe descent, she transitioned to the uneven bars event. She approached my spouse with all five fingers splayed and flexed for some specific taping situation that seemed more like a spider's web of beige athletic tape than anything else. I watched her compete on bars and was stunned; it looked like she was flying. Next was the beam and I watched her spin, flip, and dance on a singular leg atop four inches of surface, four feet in the air. She dismounted and I jumped in my seat, as there seemed to be one centimeter of clearance between her head and the end of the beam. Her final event was floor. Her routine was epic, set to marching band music, getting the most applause of all competitors across all events. I'd watched gymnastics during the Olympics every four years, but seeing it in person was wild.

If I hadn't cemented her name into my memory before the awards ceremony, I certainly did then. Every time a gymnast placed first, second, or third in the competition she stood up to be acknowledged. Lexi earned first place in more events than her teammates, including floor, and each time she stood, she put up the Black Power fist. I was struck. Not only was she incredibly brave, but she was also incredibly good at her sport. As the meet concluded, I made sure to catch Lexi's eye and give her the ubiquitous Black head nod, letting her know that she wasn't alone in that arena, and I headed out into the hall to wait for my spouse to clean up from the meet.

In the following days I learned that after that meet Lexi's coach told her that she was setting a bad example for the children and was inviting negative media coverage. I was confused. Wouldn't it make sense that others on the team and her coaches support their highest scorer, as she seemed essential to the success of the team? One might think so, but that's not how whiteness works.

. . .

OLYMPIC GYMNASTICS COMPETITIONS FOR WOMEN BEGAN IN 1928. At that time and through the mid-1900s, women were competing in their twenties and thirties. The dynamics of the field shifted dramatically in 1976. Nadia Comăneci, a fourteen-year-old Romanian gymnast coached by Béla Károlyi, was the first gymnast to score a perfect 10.0 at the Olympic games in Montreal. By the end of the games, she had earned seven scores of a perfect 10.0 and won three gold medals. She excelled on the uneven bars and balance beam, still considered to be the more *elegant* events, getting three perfect tens on each. Comăneci wasn't yet five feet tall and weighed eighty-six pounds at the time, much different from the body types of women who had been competing for the previous forty years. In a wrap-up of the 1976 Olympics, a *Sports Illustrated* author wrote:

> [Comăneci] has a lean boy's body that responds to all her demands and a Valentine face with straight, dark eyebrows that pierce it like Cupid's arrow. Her lips are faint and thin, lost beneath dusky, soul-

ful eyes that caused many of those who studied her to imagine that she must be some brooding, mysterious Carpathian princess. But those eyes: they could only express the wonder of a child examining grownups acting like children. And mystery? Intrigue? Never did any performer offer less, because all that this innocent little chimney sweep is—every bit of her—was poured out every night over the vault, atop the beam, on the bars and upon the orange mat of the Forum. There could be nothing left for her to conceal. She is, after all, 14, a mechanic's daughter from Onesti, a factory town in the mountains of Romania, who sleeps with a favorite doll, tussles with her younger brother Adrian, and has a life experience beyond her sport no larger than herself.[1]

Comăneci was an Olympics darling and is credited with popularizing the sport, shifting it to value the small, slender frames associated with graceful white girls' bodies, more than women's bodies. Her body became the standard for all female gymnasts; her body meant winning. Language used to describe her, including her lean "boy's" body, her faint and thin lips, and the multiple references of innocence, connects the gymnast to virtue and fragility. It made this women's sport one that values small, young, delicate bodies; ones that need protecting.

What is not lost on me, gymnasts, fans, and the American public is the irony in the way that USA Gymnastics, its coaches, and Larry Nassar exploited this perception. They were able to position themselves as the protectors, those who would guard the frailty and delicacy of young female gymnasts. In doing so they were able to terrorize and traumatize generations of girls for decades without consequence.

• • •

Lexi became a part of the gymnastics community at age three.

There is the cutest photo of her at about that age. She is in a blue and purple-swirl leotard standing in a line of other tiny gymnasts, curly hair pulled back into a bun, looking nervous about something and biting her lip. It's a bittersweet photo. She's an adorable kiddo, her round toddler belly leading the way. It's the only photo of her I've seen in which I know that she wasn't concerned about how to position her body for photos and trying to suck in her belly.

It's the only photo I've seen of her before she learned the value gained by conforming to white norms. Before she knew that thinness and grace meant winning. Before she learned that long-term excellence and survival in gymnastics, dominated by the appraisal of bodies, meant she needed to constrain, restrain, and restrict herself.

• • •

Lexi's experience in gymnastics illustrates the persistence of Nadia Comăneci's legacy in the sport. Lexi has shared with me that, still today, white female gymnasts are thought to naturally have the body types desired in the sport. They were born with the *lines* and *shapes* associated with the artistry so valued in the gymnastics community. As such, they're thought to excel in the so-called elegant events, which, with a nod to Comăneci's perfect tens and footprint on the sport, continue to be beam and uneven bars.

Lexi shared that Black female gymnasts are described as powerful and muscular. They are considered animalistic, she says, and easier to dismiss or label as hostile, which would be in obvious contrast to the type of gymnast who would compete in the "elegant" events. Black gymnasts are encouraged to compete on vault and floor, the power events.

The same year that Comăneci set the standards for gymnasts' bodies, Dominique Dawes was born. Dawes was the first Black person to win an individual Olympic medal in gymnastics. She medaled at the 1992, 1996, and 2000 Olympics, yet she never escaped the narrative that she didn't belong in the sport. In 1995, Maryann Hudson, a staff writer for the *Los Angeles Times*, wrote about Dawes: "There was something exceptional about Dominique Dawes early on, but still, the critics whispered. Her look wasn't quite right, some said. Maybe it was those legs, so bowed. Or those knees, so knobby. Sometimes it was her hair, too askew. But none of the critics would be bold enough to hint that a major difference in Dawes's look was her color."[2] Dawes's body was unruly; it didn't have the lines associated with white gymnasts. She was fifteen at her first Olympics, just one year older than Comăneci had been, and the language used to describe Dawes's body was in stark contrast to the way observers gushed over Comăneci and her "innocence." The same narratives that were projected upon Dawes's body continued for Gabby Douglas and Simone Biles, both, arguably, the best gymnasts of their times.[3]

The dynamic between Blackness and whiteness in gymnastics is predictable, given how we've been conditioned to appraise bodies. In supposed *contrast* to white gymnasts' elegance, Black gymnasts are portrayed as strong and powerful. This aligns with Western society's narrative of Black women being best used for our labor. We're praised for what we can do for society, not for what we bring.

Whiteness is the standard, and Black women's bodies are the farthest one could be from needing the protection that white girls command in society simply by existing.

This portrayal also aligns with the adultification of young Black girls. A report from Georgetown Law quotes coauthor Rebecca Epstein saying, "Our . . . research focused on adult attitudes and found that adults think Black girls as young as 5 need less protection and nurturing than their white peers."[4] This research provides additional evidence to support the perception that white girlhood and womanhood is socially constructed to be fragile. White supremacy has always served and protected those thought to be delicate, often to the detriment of those considered to threaten that construction.

Black bodies don't conform to the standards set by the gymnastics community. They spill outside the bounds of acceptability; they rebel against societal rules. In a sport that relies on the subjective approval and appraisal of gymnasts by primarily white judges, being able to tame a rebellious body, make it more feminine, and conform to what whiteness demands are essential to advancement in the sport. It means winning.

For Lexi, told she wasn't smart enough to get to college based on her grades alone, excelling in gymnastics to earn a scholarship was her path forward. To survive and win in a sport that values whiteness, the tools of constraint, restraint, and restriction were necessary for her. Liquid diets, supplements instead of meals, caffeine pills, and purging weren't components of an eating disorder.

It made sense to her, because "the skinny people were winning." Her tactics were essential to get the job done. To win. She and her teammates were told by their high school coach to drink lemon water with cayenne pepper to "burn the belly fat" and to take their weight and add a zero to determine how many calories they needed in a day. If she and her teammates exceeded this amount, it wasn't a problem because they could throw up the extra. No big deal.

The advice wasn't specific to her. It was generalized for all of the girls on her club team. But the outcomes were far different. While her white teammates would be seen as simply thinner, Lexi could get closer to whiteness. Closer to winning.

It wasn't about her pursuit of thinness.

It wasn't about diet culture.

It wasn't about "health."

It wasn't because she had "poor body image."

It wasn't an outcome of her personal concerns and perceptions.

It was about something much bigger than herself, something wrapped into the origins of this country.

• • •

ACCORDING TO THE FIFTH EDITION OF THE *DIAGNOSTIC AND Statistical Manual of Mental Disorders* (DSM-5), to *qualify* as having bulimia nervosa one's "**Self**-evaluation is unjustifiably influenced by body shape and weight."

For anorexia nervosa and atypical anorexia nervosa, one needs to have *intense* fear of gaining weight and be *disturbed* by one's **own** weight or shape.

As read, it implies that an individual needs to be concerned about their own body. That the diagnosis comes from an *internal* concern about weight or shape.

But.

How do we define "disturbed"? What if an individual is undisturbed by their own body, but *others* are disturbed? What if someone's self-evaluation is *justifiably* influenced by their shape and weight?

Every time Black women leave the house we're reminded of how others view our bodies. The mental and physical preparation required to venture into spaces that others wouldn't think twice about entering can be exhausting. Within family systems we receive messages about how to have a body.

Society is often disturbed by our existence, by our bodies. It makes sense that our self-evaluation be influenced by our shape and weight.

Mia knew this. She was fully aware that her Blackness had a direct impact on the direction of her career in STEM. Mia's grades were good, but she knew that she needed to be at the top of her class to compete for the same jobs as the most average of her paler classmates. She would also need a strong letter of recommendation, and for Mia it made sense to try to make herself smaller, more respectable, more palatable to survive. She had an intense fear of weight gain and was aware of her shape and weight, justifiably so. But it wasn't about a thin ideal.

As with all else, thin white cis women are centered in the ways we decide who "gets" to have an eating disorder. By constructing categories in such a way that only the frail among us fit, it ensures that only those thought to deserve protection receive it.

. . .

When the causes of eating disorders are put upon the individual and their self-perceived disturbance about their own body, we leave out all individuals about whom *society* is disturbed. When we believe that behaviors come from an internal distortion, we reinforce that only those whose existence is affirmed by white supremacy are those who get eating disorders. We also then employ individual "solutions" to systemic problems, solutions like improving one's own body image.

When I attended the aforementioned eating disorder conference in 2019, I joined a session on body image. In it the speakers, two eating disorder therapists, handed out a worksheet from Thomas Cash's Body Image Workbook, created in the 1990s. Decades later, it seems like it's still a best practice. The worksheet is supposed to be used with eating disorder clients to build cognitive dissonance; to help them realize that what they think to be true about their bodies is false, it's an assumption. Conference participants were told to fill it out individually so we could discuss as a large group. The worksheet asks clients to rate their own appearance "assumptions" on a scale of 1 to 5 for how true they believe each statement to be. This worksheet asks ten questions, including the following:

- "By controlling my appearance I can control my social and emotional health."
- "My appearance is responsible for much of what has happened to me in my life."
- "The only way I could ever like my looks is to change them."[5]

I sat there and read through it and waited until the large group discussion began before raising my hand. "Do you use this worksheet with your clients who aren't thin cis non-disabled white women?" I asked.

Indeed they do, I was told.

"But these aren't assumptions for many of us. They're realities and it seems quite dismissive of lived experiences," I followed up. The speaker told me that this tool has been in use for decades; it's considered best practice. The end. I walked out; I needed a break.

These worksheet questions, like the entirety of one-on-one eating disorder treatment interventions, reinforce the notion that beliefs about our bodies exist only in our heads. They're assumptions.

But.

It is not an "assumption" for many of us whose body narrative doesn't conform to what whiteness demands that our "appearance is responsible for much of what has happened to [us in our lives]."

As fat people and Black women are assigned largesse, restraining and restricting with attempts to shrink into something more palatable may improve "social and emotional health."

Marginalized folks are treated with more dignity and respect when we conform to societal body norms and expectations. With positive feedback and affirmation received from views warped by white supremacy, we may find that we "like our looks." Mia and Lexi saw this, through a lens defined by whiteness.

The modalities and institutions of the eating disorder field, similar to the gymnastics institutions, uphold the idea that only delicate, thin white women belong. The prioritized members are those whose only reason to be disturbed by their bodies is one of self-perception because they naturally have the lines and shapes that follow the rules we've collectively agreed upon for *good* bodies.

• • •

IN THE WEEK FOLLOWING THE FIRST UC DAVIS HOME MEET, I walked over to the gymnastics gym to wait for my spouse to pack up all of the treatment and rehab equipment after practice. I watched Lexi get wrapped up in bags of ice and noticed the tears in her eyes, welling but fully restrained.

I didn't know if I should say something.

I didn't know if I would make it worse.

Hell, I didn't know how to make a proper introduction to a twenty-year-old. Would she even want to talk to me?

Welp, I decided to find out.

I took a deep breath and invited her to sit on the bench outside the practice gym. A couple tears broke free and spilled down her cheeks. The criticism, gaslighting, and outright bullying from her teammates and coaches were too much.

I sat there, silent.

I hadn't mentored anyone before and didn't know what it looked like. Was I supposed to *do* something?

All I remember asking was, "How can I support you?"

Four years later, we recalled how we started talking, and she said of that first meeting, "It wasn't great. I was pretty defensive and said I didn't need any support. I think I said 'I'm fine.'" She was conditioned, as all athletes and all Black women, to be strong, independent, and not rely on others for support.

On the bench outside the gym that first day we met, Lexi wasn't able to talk about feelings. The next few times we connected, she said that "we barely talked about anything because I was like, 'Uh-oh' about talking about feelings." She wasn't ever afforded the capacity to have emotions; her goal was to win.

Things shifted on February 11, 2017, when her team competed at the Air Force Academy, north of Colorado Springs, Colorado. Her silent protest there was a reminder that peaceful protest can bring violence. She recalled in a 2020 Instagram post:

> I was called up as first place and raised my fist into the air, lowered my head, and had a solemn look on my face. Winning gave me the platform to honor those lost to police brutality. . . . When I looked up I saw the parents of a gymnast in the stands mocking me and making faces. This continued as I was called up for every award. . . . Awards ended and I thought I should go address the parents so that I could explain what my protest was about. I asked if they understood the protest and if they would like to know more. The response was "I'm NOT a RACIST, how dare you." . . . I was pulled away by my coaches and team because "I had started a conflict." My Black body in a sparkling leotard is still threatening.[6]

It was the last time some of her teammates would talk to her that year.

In a sport dominated by thin, delicate white women, Lexi's very existence, her *body*, was dangerous and needed containment. Later, Lexi overheard her coach ask one of the Black track-and-field coaches how to "calm her down and tone down her protest." She met with the athletic director multiple times during and after that violent season and was never informed she had the option to report this abuse officially outside of Athletics and to campus authorities. Her coach was protected, whiteness was protected, and he continued to coach Black athletes.

Assumed to handle pain with poise and composure, Lexi was never offered the support she needed. Whereas the department would have likely rallied behind a white athlete who was being bullied and offered her resources, I was the one to connect Lexi to a Black therapist on campus.

Following the meet at the Air Force Academy was the closest I'd ever been to having a momma bear moment. I went from casually supportive, letting Lexi lead the process, to outright rage and decided to do something about it. I began networking among the UC Davis campus and alumni. Lexi found incredible support among students at the Cross Cultural Center and its staff. I was able to connect her to Black staff and faculty to support her, as well as community members in Davis and Sacramento. Fans started coming out to gymnastic meets and would take photos and ask for autographs. Each time, Lexi's face showed that she was just as surprised and flattered. Shana joined me and others with our butts in chairs or standing with fists in the air during the national anthem.

This culminated in Lexi's own cheering section at the home meet against the Air Force Academy in March of that year. When standing up to accept her awards, her fist flying high into the air, the fans yelling even louder than before, her smile was so wide and so bright it lit the arena.

Lexi was the best and most decorated gymnast on that team, breaking multiple long-held school records. Yet after her silent

protest, she wasn't voted team captain for her senior year; a sopho-
more was voted captain instead. She wasn't a leader in the eyes of
her team. She was too much, yet not enough.

It wasn't until the summer of 2020 that her story got the attention it deserved. She was in her first year of vet school in London and
fielding interview requests from the States. She put her experiences
on Instagram, and during the time that people were most invested
in Black women's well-being, people wanted to know more about
her story. She heard from the chancellor over social media who was
supportive, though at the same time the Athletics Department was
attempting damage control. Lexi was finally offered the opportunity
to report what had happened to the university's harassment and discrimination office, something she hadn't known was an option. A
UC Davis campus investigation was opened, and closed, with "in-
conclusive findings" of harassment or discrimination. Of course.
She was disregarded and discarded from UC Davis once again. She
was the one to experience the consequences of her coaches' and
teammates' abuse while they were free to live their best, basic lives.

• • •

LEXI WAS GASLIGHTED ABOUT HER EXPERIENCE. HER COACH TOLD
her that racism is no longer alive. She was denied body autonomy,
made to hug a teammate and "make up" after the teammate called
Lexi ghetto. The violence and the vitriol Lexi experienced in protest,
the bullying, ostracizing, and shaming from teammates and coaches,
were unacceptable, yet also typical for Black women when we dare
to question the status quo and draw attention to the legacy of chattel
slavery in the United States.

Day-to-day existence in societies that have formed social constructions and caste distinctions that define the difference between life and death is traumatic.

A few years out of my didactic training I was working in college health. I needed to learn about eating disorders, and fast. From talking with therapists and reading books from the nineties that were recommended to me I learned that trauma can contribute to the development of an eating disorder. Yet the discussion about trauma typically extended only to physical, psychological, and sexual trauma. Nothing I read addressed the trauma of societal violence and oppression. Dietitians and, in my experience, therapists don't learn how intergenerational trauma and colonization impact the ways we eat. We don't learn about how the legacies of enslavement and Jim Crow impact the development of constraint, restraint, and restriction.

Restriction reduces cognitive functioning, which can lead to numbed feelings and minimized emotional responses. Starvation reduces both the gray and white matter in the brain.[7] As such, starving is an effective coping strategy for trauma.

Lexi starved herself for eight years.

$\bullet\ \bullet\ \bullet$

LEXI AND I MET WEEKLY FROM MARCH TO JUNE OF 2017 OUTSIDE of the UC Davis Student Community Center, where I introduced her to the Black students and staff who had supported her protest. We met there because the majority of people who gathered in the building and outside in the courtyard were folks of color; we didn't get the raised eyebrows and surprised glances that being Black women on the UC Davis campus would elicit.

Each week we bought coffee from the CoHo, a student-run eatery where I had worked for three years as a student. Lexi and I would save up our quarters, nickels, and dimes all week so we could get the cash discount; we both can't resist a deal. It was here, at the round metal tables with attached metal chairs and umbrellas, that we talked politics, activism, and her classes. I'd ask her about the gender performance of gymnastics and the history of glitter, bows, and fake smiles in the sport. I also got updates on how her team, coaches, and the Athletics Department were treating her. When I'd try to delve into anything deeper that involved feelings, I'd always preface it with, "I know you don't have feelings . . . and . . ." It was often a futile attempt and I needed to accept it just wasn't our time to connect on such a level.

If Lexi had been eating enough food, the trauma and pain of systemic and everyday racism would have been available for her to feel. She wouldn't have been able to get through her season, and she wouldn't have been able to get through her academic course load.

She wouldn't have been able to survive.

. . .

I OFTEN GET THE QUESTION FROM CLINICIANS, "HOW DO WE MAKE Black women buy in to the fact that they have an eating disorder?" Which implies these clinicians can only support their clients if clients see themselves as checking all of the boxes, see themselves as what an eating disorder "looks like," and find themselves endorsing the diagnostic criteria.

But.

How could a client have an eating disorder if they literally don't fit the diagnosis?

How could a client have an eating disorder if all assessment tools, resources, interventions, research, and representation in clinicians available aren't meant to serve them?

To imply that only when Black women accept an eating disorder diagnosis are we deserving enough to receive treatment upholds the idea of whiteness as the model, the norm, and inherently implies that a clinician would treat a Black woman with an eating disorder with the same framing as they would treat a white woman.

Because the eating disorder field has actively kept Black women and other marginalized individuals out of the research, frameworks, modalities, and clinical positions, I'm not going to ask that we be squeezed into a paradigm that was never meant to hold us, even though we've been in this country since its inception. I'm not going to use language in which Black women don't see ourselves.

I'm going to name constriction, restriction, restraint, and *survival* as such, rather than disordered.

I'm not going to *treat* the individual, when the problem is not their own. I don't need to diagnose a client in order to help them heal.

I'm not going to pathologize the ways in which some Black women have organized their lives to be safer. Not doing so provides an opportunity for a broader discussion and multiple truths. We can be expansive in our language and create opportunities for other folks who don't fall into the very narrow category of what an eating disorder "looks like" to do the same.

. . .

TODAY, LEXI IS IN VET SCHOOL AT THE ROYAL VETERINARY College of London. As of this writing, it is the number one vet school in the world. This, as her mentor, is a giant middle finger to the chorus of people at UC Davis who told her that she wasn't smart enough for vet school, and that only by using her Black body and aligning with whiteness would she get anywhere in life. Following the recognition she received during her junior year, she earned a 4.0 GPA going forward. As soon as people believed in her beyond her labor and offered support, she believed in herself. She was always more than enough, and I hope now she knows it.

She is now one of about five Black students in her class. She doesn't wear a leotard anymore, but she remains concerned about her appearance. She remains diligent about sucking in her belly, now doing so in scrubs. She received top marks at university during her first year and I couldn't be prouder.

She attended school remotely during the UK's COVID lock-downs and stayed with me and my spouse, as all of her flatmates had left the city and she experienced great personal loss. While she was here, more than ever, I was flexible with food and never said anything disparaging about my body. Weeks into her stay with us, we were sitting across from each other at the dinner table and I asked her about this. She told me that if I had been restricting or restraining myself, it wouldn't have triggered her; instead it would have felt normal, familiar for her. She thought it was weird that I wasn't trying to lose weight. We talked a bit more about eating food and as we wrapped that conversation, she told me that "it would have been easier if you were a kale and quinoa dietitian." She thought it would have been "easier than having to discuss this with you" and talk about "a way through." She wouldn't have to sit with the reflections about her restriction and restraint; she wouldn't have had to deal with feelings.

She told me the damage is done.

I know.

It's too much work for her to change her mindset now. Vet school is hard, and so is surviving in the Western world as a Black woman. She tells me that if restraining and restricting make it even a little easier to exist, then it's worth it, at least right now.

She's right. I see this in my clients all the time. And it still hurts to see it in her.

There is agency to be gained in harming ourselves before others are able to do so. By conforming before anyone tells us that we don't belong.

There is autonomy to be reclaimed by choosing what will happen to our bodies. By constraining ourselves before others can tell us that we're too much.

Some of us might find a way to survive in a society that wants us dead or discarded by changing the appearance of our bodies. "Recovery" from what would be deemed an eating disorder in thin white women risks far more than weight gain for Black women.

This is just one of the binds in which we find ourselves. There is no easy path forward when it comes to our bodies.

PART 2

"SOLUTIONS":
HAVING A BODY IS HARD

chapter five

Feeling Good as Hell: Body Toxitivity

HAVING A BODY IS HARD.

A colleague of mine describes it as an inconvenience. I agree. A body needs tending. It requires feeding, watering, sleep, washing, and getting it from point A to point B, however far that is. Every day.

All of this can be overwhelming, the degree to which depends on circumstance and experience.

Having a body is so hard that, as a society, we actively disconnect ourselves and others from the experience. We say things like "people *in* bodies" rather than "people"; it's an often hostile occupation. We say "people *with* bodies." To get more specific, we say "people in [adjective] bodies" versus "[adjective] people." At times

I've used this language in this book. It's hard in Western society to stay connected, or, as some folks will say, embodied. We separate people from their bodies, as if somehow the person is only their brain or their intellect and personality, and just happens to have a body attached.

We might do this in order to distance someone from their experience of body-based societal violence to indicate that we see them as something other than their body, perhaps similar to "I don't see color."

We might say, "I live in a [adjective] body" versus "my [adjective] body" or even "*me*" with intentions to distance ourselves from the narratives written about our body. I also see it from those who try to distance themselves from their privilege. Saying "I live in a white/thin/cis/healthy body" rather than "I'm a white/thin/cis/non-disabled person" can serve as a tool for those trying to separate our lived experience and inherent advantage of privilege from who we truly are "on the inside."

Meat suits are complicated.

For some, existing separately from their body is an excellent survival strategy. Staying in our body can be hard for many of us, especially those who have experienced trauma. Leaving the body and existing solely in the brain is a safe way not to feel anything at all.

Existing as a brain-only ball of cells can be a way to get us out the door and to exist outside of the assignments of race, gender, ability, clothing, and so on. If we let everything roll off our back, like a turtle, we don't have to sit with the realities that come with being what society assigns to us via our body. We can exist as something other than ourselves, something outside of ourselves. We can have this weird, fleshy onesie that exists below the neck but that doesn't have anything to do with who we truly are.

Distancing ourselves is one tool to survive the inconvenience, and violence, of having a body.

· · ·

OTHERS TAKE A DIFFERENT APPROACH. THEY PUT A POSITIVE SPIN on the experience. Body positivity is one way to reframe the realities we experience. We can *choose* to be positive about our bodies and embark on the journey to do so. "Love your body, LIVE your life!" reads the Body Positive's introduction to their main tenets. The Bay Area organization asks website visitors to "Imagine a world where people in all bodies are able to reclaim their health, beauty, and confidence to live full, happy lives." After all, who doesn't want to do that? And I was all in for this message in the early 2010s. They believed in their message so strongly that the org was running clinical trials to find whether their model was effective in addressing the "health crisis" of eating disorders. The founders are in the eating disorder community and offer "freedom from suffocating societal messages that keep people in a perpetual struggle with their bodies." It does sound positive.

For some, body positivity is seen as a movement; for others it feels like a mandate, a societal expectation that we can somehow transcend the lessons we've learned from society and put a positive spin on what it's like to exist under white supremacy. If only we could change the way we *think*, then it will be easier to navigate the world with the bodies we have. And, to be clear, it is possible for some people to do so. For those with more privilege than others, changing a mindset really will result in living a happy life. For others, it is much more complex.

Body positivity also locates the problem on the individual and confers a responsibility to think your way to positivity and happiness. If society won't let us live in peace, the opportunity to think our way to "liberation" offers a way out. It's something that we can do as singular, solitary people on a planet of billions.

In America, we cling to rugged individualism.

We love a bootstrap solution.

We look for agency in situations that seem impossible to overcome.

White supremacy culture and capitalism have conditioned us to focus on ourselves and to disconnect from systemic concerns. Individualism is an integral part of the American dream. Everyone can make it if we only try hard enough and focus our (positive) energy on ourselves! The assumption that we can think ourselves into feeling like we have a "good" body if we work hard enough is consistent with this conditioning. The people pitching us the "me" solution for something that is a "we" problem are capitalizing on our willingness to do individual work. They also don't tend to acknowledge that there are inherently folks for whom positivity will come easier and those for whom it may be impossible.

Indeed, one can buy workbooks and journals that promise a "lighthearted approach," one that is "playful and empowering," where one can simply "let go of judgment and shame and replace it with love and appreciation." Similar to the conversations of body liberation.

For some, journaling and body positivity *will* be enough.

• • •

IN 2019, BODY POSITIVITY HIT NEW HEIGHTS AS MORE AND MORE people, particularly women, were taking up literal space in the spotlight. The most prominent, or most discussed, was Lizzo herself.

Lizzo, who debuted with a major label in 2016, became a household name in 2019 for her lyrics, flute playing, twerking, and, as much as if not more, for being an unapologetic fat Black woman.

Lizzo took up space as a musical artist. Leading up to the release of her album *Cuz I Love You*, she posted photos of herself on Instagram, naked before the camera, one of which is featured on her album cover. Lizzo shared many candid photos of herself wearing minimal garments, if any at all. The world was also invited to view videos of her amazing twerking via social media. Lizzo's self-love message to her followers at the time was clear.

In the before-times, when sold-out stadium concerts were routine, the famous *bop* star's concerts were a must-see for those getting inspiration from Lizzo's unapologetic abundance. Thousands of white women got their whole life from her *Cuz I Love You* tour. They would jump up and down with unrhythmic fervor while participating in an enthusiastic call-and-response to one of Lizzo's most popular songs.

"Baby, how you feeling?"

"Feeling good as hell!"

Her overwhelming appeal to white women was one of the many critiques she received from Black folks. "Yeah, there's hella white people at my shows," she asserts. "What am I gonna do, turn them away? My music is for everybody," she responded in a feature with *Rolling Stone*.[1]*

The people were ready for Lizzo. She soared to the top of the charts and into millions of hearts. Celebrities and influencers had been telling us to unapologetically love our bodies for decades, and Lizzo, a fat Black woman, seemed to be living this truth. Fans and haters alike saw someone who was openly rebelling against society's unwritten rules to keep fat people covered and classy at all times. Her online presence and persona were one giant middle finger to the body norms of this country. Her 2019 Cuz I Love You tour was so popular, it was extended to Cuz I Love You Too, which took her into early 2020. She was performing almost every week, crossing continents for her shows.

Twenty-twenty was a Hard Year. It sucked for so many of us for so many reasons, and Lizzo was transparent about this, telling us via Instagram that in November 2020 "I drank a lot, I ate a lot of spicy things and things that fucked my stomach up."[2] She decided to change things up for herself and try something that may make her feel better. She drank smoothies, water, and tea and ate protein bars, apples, peanut butter, and pickles (and nothing else) and soaked herself in herbs for ten straight days.

She and author J. J. Smith called these choices a "smoothie detox." This dietitian called it completely understandable given the ridiculously incomplete and misleading information about how to eat food that comes at us daily and how even celebrities are subject to marketing.

---

* Lizzo addresses this in her song "Rumors": "They don't know I do it for the culture / god damn."

The People of the Internet, however, called it an absolute betrayal.

The backlash was swift and ferocious. Coming from the same women who were getting their whole lives from Lizzo, there was now an outpouring of shaming and an immediate conflation of said "cleanse" with the (incorrect) assumption that Lizzo was doing this for weight loss after being their beacon of body positivity and sharing the message to love their bodies the way they are.

The same group of people who had staunchly defended Lizzo's right to eat anything she wanted after she was trolled by fatphobic haters for eating burritos and burgers suddenly couldn't handle unapologetic smoothie drinking.

Even those in my field who, time and time again, proclaim that eating a burger doesn't lead to automatic weight gain provided dissertations about how drinking smoothies for ten days means one is invested in intentional weight loss.*

The same people on the internet who had defended Lizzo against Jillian Michaels for assigning disease to Lizzo's body were attacking Lizzo for using a blender.†

Social media was abuzz with heartbroken fans believing that their body positive fave wanted to lose weight. This was personal: Lizzo had broken their trust. There were entire think pieces on social media, mostly from non-Black individuals. Those in the eating

---

* Do people use J. J. Smith's smoothies to drop the fifteen pounds that one of her books promises? Yup. Does that mean Lizzo did? Nope.
(Even if she did, she owes you nothing.)

† Quote from Michaels, who can fuck all the way off: "Why aren't we celebrating her music? 'Cause it isn't gonna be awesome if she gets diabetes" (Lisa France, "Jillian Michaels Slammed for Comments About Lizzo's Weight," CNN Entertainment, January 9, 2020, https://www.cnn.com/2020/01/09/entertainment/jillian-michaels-lizzo-weight-trnd/index.html).

disorder and dietetics fields and those in the body positivity community had heralded Lizzo as a leader in their personal quests to feel better about their bodies and to have clients feel better about themselves. They now sought justice. People shared self-care tips for when our fat faves go on a smoothie cleanse.

A very thin and extremely popular non-Black body positivity influencer wrote about her own experiences "cleansing" herself that had put her in the hospital, as a cautionary tale for her fans. This influencer had done her own cleanse to further chase the thin ideal and was concerned that others would be inspired to start drinking smoothies and eating protein bars, peanut butter, and pickles too. And still, I hadn't seen anything from Lizzo about wanting to lose weight.

People were concern-trolling Lizzo with gusto, which, for an unapologetic and abundant fat Black woman, was nothing new. This time, though, those who previously defended Lizzo's right to eat anything she damn well pleased were now the ones policing her eating. This change in dynamics revealed that there are limits to the body positive movement and unspoken community guidelines.

Lizzo had not only broken the BoPo rules, she had offended her fans. She went from pedestal to pariah overnight. Lizzo, clearly, did not know how to be body positive. Lizzo had somehow been assigned the position of being her fans' body positivity Mammy. They had found comfort in her presence and believed her to be *warm, smart, hardworking,* and *loyal.* These women needed Lizzo to act in accord with their own needs. It seemed like she existed only to make these women feel better about their bodies: if a fat Black woman could find a way to love her body, then certainly they could too. These "fans" had entered into a one-way relationship with Lizzo and somehow began expecting things of someone who owed them nothing.

This was how I was reading the situation, but I was curious about how younger fat Black women were perceiving the smoothie-pocalypse. A year later, I reached out to Larrolyn (Larri) Parms Ford, someone I'd connected with during time spent in fat-positive spaces in Oakland. It had been years since we chatted; she'd gone off to grad school and returned. We caught up via Zoom and were able to pinpoint the first time we were in the same space. It was in the mid-2010s, during a panel at Mills College in Oakland titled "When Body Positivity Is Not Enough: Fat Liberation." Larri says it was at that panel that she recognized the false promises in positivity.

Larri follows Lizzo on TikTok, on which Lizzo is a regular content creator, posting daily updates about her life, including wild and wacky food combinations she tries, exercise she does, and for ten days in late 2020, the smoothies she drank. I asked Larri about Lizzo and the cleanse debacle and her first response was, "I felt so bad for her, and I saw it coming." Larri noted that the branding Lizzo had done on TikTok was very different from that on Instagram. On TikTok, people got daily insights into what food, including vegetables, Lizzo was eating, and followers got to watch her hard workouts. On Instagram, Lizzo chose more of the body positive–focused pictures and videos and more curated content. Larri noticed that the backlash came when Lizzo decided to put her smoothies on Instagram, something that wasn't consistent with her branding message on that platform. I asked Larri if she cared about Lizzo's smoothies or exercise. Larri absolutely did not, "This makes complete sense to me." She said that Lizzo is an influencer and of course companies seek her out hoping she will advertise their products. Larri assumed that the smoothie book author approached Lizzo with an offer and asked Lizzo to promote it if she liked it; no more, no less, "it's influencer life." But whatever reason Lizzo decided to work with J. J. Smith doesn't matter to Larri, "that doesn't change Lizzo." Larri believes that Lizzo didn't want to be thin and knows that Lizzo doesn't disparage fatness. Lizzo is still going to be fine being fat. Larri holds the many dimensions to Lizzo and the complex life she leads. Larri loves seeing an unapologetic fat Black woman living her best life. And that's all.

· · ·

Even though Lizzo told us via Instagram, "I detoxed my body and I'm still fat. I love my body and I'm still fat. I'm beautiful and I'm still fat. These things are not mutually exclusive,"[3] the idea that a body positive influencer must behave in a certain way was out there. Apparently, there is a right way and a wrong way, a binary to uphold. Unapologetically eating donuts, burgers, and burritos is the Right Way; drinking smoothies in public is the Wrong Way.

During this hysteria, Lizzo bothered to take time to dignify the BoPo police by responding, "I did the 10-day smoothie detox, and, as you know, I would normally be so afraid and ashamed to post things like this online, because I feel like, as a big girl, people just expect if you are doing something for health, you're doing it for, like, a dramatic weight loss, and that is not the case." Indeed.

I decided to discuss it with the internet:

On the mammification of Black women.

Black women do not exist to make white women feel better about themselves and their bodies. Black women may have been instrumental in Your healing, we are still trying to get ours.

If y'all . . . feel the need to take self-care because a Black woman chose to drink smoothies for a while, because she had a sh*t month, please ask why this feels personal. As you're focused on Self-Care in this moment . . . reflect on the care that Black women have been denied for centuries.

Why were folks making it about themselves? I asked them, "[Lizzo's] good boo, what about you?"

Black women, especially fat women, don't owe us anything.

Lizzo is rewriting the narrative of what it looks like to be more than one thing.

* * *

IN 2021, WHILE EATING A DIPPED CONE FROM DAIRY QUEEN, I asked Shana about Lizzo. She shared that she had not caught the smoothie-gate scandal of late 2020 but agreed that Lizzo had fallen from her BoPo pedestal. In fact, Shana noticed it start almost a year earlier.

In early December 2019, with a night off from touring, Lizzo attended an NBA Lakers game wearing an oversized black T-shirt with an oval cutout in the back that revealed her butt and her black thong underwear. Lizzo had a courtside seat and during the game, one of her songs, "Juice," started playing and she bopped out of her seat and started dancing; the crowd went wild. When she turned around with her back to the camera and began twerking, the party was over.

The internet had Big Thoughts about her clothing choices, again on par with any Black woman's existence in the public eye. She wasn't following the rules for both fat people's and Black women's unwritten rules of respectability. She was too much.

All of the professional critics swore up and down that their assessment wasn't because Lizzo was fat, nor because she was Black.[*]

The issue? It was "indecent." There were "innocent families" there.[4] What does that even mean? Where do the guilty families congregate? Maybe they're watching red carpet premieres and galas where thinner and less melanated women are praised for their sheer and sparkly fashion choices, and where one can regularly find a Kardashian or a Jenner wearing next to nothing. Perhaps the guilty families are on the California, Florida, and international beaches where thong swimsuit bottoms are commonplace and backsides are no big deal? I'd say it's confusing, but unfortunately it's predictable. Not only had Lizzo become too positive, but she was also subject to what respectability demands.

Lizzo's rear end also posed an existential crisis for the acceptance of the BoPo community at large. "Is Lizzo Taking Body Positivity Too Far?!"[5] was a common headline and sentiment. The question itself underscores that there is a limit to how much skin someone should show and how positive someone should be.

---

[*] Oh no, misogynoir and anti-fatness were not at play, they just weren't.

Lizzo met the line that one should not cross and apparently did a deep dive over it.

Look, if we want to count the inch-for-inch ratio of fabric to skin, there was more skin showing on the Lakers dancers than on Lizzo. The criticism was most certainly about Lizzo's fatness and Blackness.

The body positivity community and everyone else came for Lizzo, in the end. If BoPo isn't for Lizzo, who is it for?

· · ·

IN THE 2010S, THE EATING DISORDER COMMUNITY WAS LOOKING to make body positivity and body image improvement curricula "evidence-based." In addition to the research Bay Area–based Body Positive was doing, Eugene, Oregon–based Dr. Eric Stice and fellow researchers were researching the Body Project, the curriculum UC Davis was using about which I had expressed my concerns. It promises that a "reduction in thin-ideal internalization should result in improved body satisfaction and improved mood, reduced use of unhealthy weight-control behaviors, and decreased binge eating and other eating disorder symptoms."[6] Again, the *thin ideal* is the primary problem centered in the research.

I was adjacent to the initial clinical trial for the Body Project while working at the University of Oregon. In the early 2010s, a few of the peer health students I supervised participated in the pilot. At the time, I was talking about body positivity to my clients and was excited to be involved in something that addressed it directly. I was still newer to eating disorder care and was constantly told "Body image is the first thing that influences eating disorder development and both the last and hardest thing to work on in recovery" by well-meaning colleagues, so I figured that the project was the path to recovery for everyone at that time. I eventually realized that the project reinforced the same norms about eating disorder clients, especially in the use of "fat talk" in its curriculum. Examples of fat talk and phrases that people should not use include:

- "No one will date me if I don't drop a few pounds."
- "I'm so fat."
- "I'm trying to get rid of everything that jiggles."
- "My thighs are so big."
- "I hate my flat chest."

Without dissecting these word for word, I will say that these statements could absolutely be a neutral reality for fat folks or valid concerns in US society for fat and trans and nonbinary folks—all of which should not be problematized. And the use of the phrase *fat talk* itself as a Bad Thing is inherently anti-fat and harmful. Unfortunately, this makes sense, because what was lost among the fine print of the project's aims was that it is both an eating disorder *and* an "obesity" prevention intervention. Stice was of the belief that one could prevent teens and young women from ever getting fat by preventing the weight loss–regain cycle that happens to people who restrict food. The nod to "reduced use of unhealthy weight-control behavior, and decreased binge eating" in the project description is code for this idea. The Body Project wasn't promoting cognitive dissonance; it was erasing the existence of those they didn't believe should be allowed to have an eating disorder. Eating disorder treatment providers and researchers like to think they "straddle the fence" between "obesity" prevention and eating disorder prevention, as if the two could coexist anywhere in the same solar system. The field will always be about protecting and promoting thinness.

Years later, when I'd returned to UC Davis and expressed my concerns about the Body Project and its use of "fat talk" and the thin/healthy ideal for body expectations, you'll recall I was met with Big Feelings. One of the therapists was deeply, emotionally tied to the project and wasn't willing to give it up. She noted that Stice and his researchers were developing a "more inclusive" curriculum that would eliminate my concerns.

The EVERYbody Project was piloted, and in 2021 they published their research. I requested the journal article and was prepared to dig into the nuances and decipher any coded language to find whether the eating disorder field was moving in a positive direction. I didn't need to interpret anything; it was written clearly. In the 2021 paper the authors state, "One limitation of the current research is that we did not have an adequate sample size in either trial to examine the impact of the EVERYbody Project on specific identity groups. . . . Further, many of the measures used in these studies have not been normed or validated on gender-expansive individuals, and they may not capture the unique body image issues related to both gender and weight or shape."[7]

Additionally, "A number of negative impacts of the EVERYbody Project also were identified. Five out of seven participants (ten separate mentions) said that there was little visible diversity in their group, and they did not want to speak for their entire identity group or risk being tokenized. Participants also said that, at times, the conversation was uncomfortable (four out of seven participants). Some participants also reported that they had to assess the group's openness and acceptance before they shared (three out of seven participants shared this)." Good, the authors acknowledged the limitations of the intervention, so we could go back to square one and center those whose bodies weren't worthy of the initial intervention.

And yet. And YET:

"The EVERYbody Project appears to be a feasible and acceptable dissonance-based, gender-inclusive, diversity-focused body image intervention for universal college student audiences."[8] And this paper and its conclusion were peer reviewed; it was "evidence-based"; it was still a best practice.

Of course. Body image "best practices" and societal norms will always serve the interests of thin cis white women.

In her book *Fattily Ever After*, Stephanie Yeboah, a fat Black womxn from the UK, tells us, "The truth is, body positivity is for white womxn. White female bodies being safe is paramount to upholding white supremacy." Yeboah's statement directly addresses these "best practices" and the ways we still prioritize and protect those for whom the rules about bodies are written.

There are those who can lean in and do this positivity work who will not only feel better about themselves but also will feel safer existing in society. Distilling messages to positivity and beauty will not change societal narratives. If society is able to expand our beliefs about desirability to include people larger than a size 8, white women will become more desirable and, inherently, safer. When we look at white supremacy and the ways in which it functions, keeping white women desirable and powerful while also preserving the idea of their frailty and vulnerability, at any size, whiteness continues to win.

. . .

"I . . . DON'T CONSIDER MYSELF BODY POSITIVE BECAUSE I FEEL like body positivity is such a weird word. . . . I don't know, I just, I hate that there's a name for, like, not hating a part of who you are, do you know what I'm sayin'? Like, it's *insane* that there's a word for it."

Emmy-nominated *Nailed It* host Nicole Byer shared these thoughts with Sam Sanders during a 2020 podcast interview for an episode of *It's Been a Minute.*[9] The two discussed Byer's book *#VERYFAT #VERYBRAVE: The Fat Girl's Guide to Being #Brave and Not a Dejected, Melancholy, Down-in-the-Dumps Weeping Fat Girl in a Bikini* and what it was like for her to take pictures of herself laughing all over Southern California wearing a hundred different bikinis.

Some of my fat clients who are looking to see themselves reflected in pop culture lament that most fat influencers are often in finely curated outfits, giving a sultry vibe on Instagram, have a body positive message, perhaps a life lesson to share, and are influencers *because* they're fat. My clients are looking for someone who has an identity outside of the narratives assigned to their body, someone who is known for who they are, and who is also fat. Nicole Byer seems to resonate. She's super rad, super funny, and her Instagram page shows someone living her best life.

I was initially cautious to recommend her book because my clients had shared that they'd seen enough curated photos of fat influencers with hourglass figures in bikinis and hadn't found them helpful. I was worried this book would be more of the same. I finally picked it up after a fat client told me it had changed her

life. The client had high amounts of body-related distress and just
didn't see a way she could live her life without losing weight. After
reading Byer's book, she felt much different. Byer was a talented,
funny fat woman; she wasn't an influencer because she was fat.
The client appreciated how Byer approached the idea of fat people
being "so brave" and inspirational for daring to wear something
that shows their skin. Byer turned #verybrave on its head with
photos of her in bikinis alongside commentary critiquing the idea
that fat people are brave just for existing. My clients were here for
it. In one photo, Byer is wearing a tropical-print bikini on an LA
rooftop watering a very dead garden with the caption "#veryfat
#verybrave while watering the graveyard of plants I savagely ate
because there was nothing left in the fridge." In the same plant
graveyard she is also pictured drinking from a hose because "I'm
#veryfat, so I have to drink a lot of water to hydrate my big, nasty
body, and the easiest way to do it is with a hose." Throughout
the book Byer seems to be having a great time getting her photos
taken; her joy was captured and it shone through.

Byer's known for being funny, learning to roller skate during
quarantine, pole dancing, and speaking off the cuff, and she is de-
cidedly not safe for work. In one episode of her podcast, *Best Friends*,
which she hosts with Sasheer Zamata, Byer shares her 2022 travel
plans and plans to find a man. In the same podcast episode, she also
shares that she needs to find a good tailor who can turn the three
pairs of jeans she just bought into one pair for her, like it's a regular
Thursday thing; NBD. I recommended the book to additional clients, one of whom said, "Wow, that's my body!" Byer doesn't have
the hourglass figure popularized on Instagram. My clients check her
out and read her book, and this does the work for them that two

other books, a workbook, a movie, and influencers hadn't been able to do: to see what it's like to live a fun life as a fat person.

After reading Byer's book the client who initially shared it with me was so relieved to see that she could be a fat person and live her best life. It wasn't going to be easy—she would still need therapy to support her with the realities of anti-fatness—but the book had given her a sense of possibility. She became an advocate for addressing weight stigma in her academic program. She no longer had the food-related distress and desperate need to lose weight as she had before.

In the *It's Been a Minute* interview, Byer told us why she wanted to write the book: "I wanted to write a book about fat ladies—because I am one. Not curvy, not plus-size, not big-boned, not fluffy, not phat. I'm FAT. I'm a fat lady who loves wearing bikinis. Which is #verybrave in our culture today."[10]

She continued, "It's weird when people are like 'Nicole, you're so body positive' and I'm like 'No, I just don't hate the body I'm in because the world is already really hard.'" Byer is rewriting the narrative of what it means to be #brave and inspiring others to do the same.

● ● ●

PUSHING POSITIVITY ABOUT HOW WE FEEL AND THINK LIMITS THE responsibility of society to make any cultural shifts. The erasure from the narrative of fat people, trans people, disabled people, chronically ill people, undesirable people, and those for whom these identities intersect makes sense.

Clinicians end up gaslighting clients when we talk to them about positivity and say that we can help them to think themselves into feeling safer in their body. It creates a dynamic in which clinicians don't hear what our clients are saying and disregard the realities that don't lend themselves to positivity. I texted Lexi to ask her if body positivity ever resonated with her and she replied, "Nooppppeeee. It's like self-care bubble bath—unrealistic."

I asked a Black nonbinary friend of mine who was going through eating disorder recovery what they thought about how eating disorder clinicians on social media talked about body positivity. They told me that it was "A lot of thin white people making a lot of noise. . . . As I'm going through recovery, as I'm weight restoring . . . hearing a lot of thin white people saying 'it's okay to be the size you are.'" This was not true for them.

I asked another Black friend about whether body positivity had been helpful in her eating disorder recovery. She gave a quick no and added that "I'm not white, I'm not straight," so body positivity wasn't even something she considered; she found it more helpful to look at the demographics of the queer community, with its more diverse body types and gender presentation. She also likens body positivity to "Live, Laugh, Love": "It's cute, but, what does it stand for?"

On the Zoom call I had with Shana, Ifasina, and Fresh, I first asked them about body positivity and if it had been helpful for them. All three agreed that body positivity had been a good gateway to eventually getting to fat activism and fat liberation work; it worked for them, until it didn't. Shana spoke to my friend's query: "Yeah, it's completely meaningless. That's why it works. . . . I just feel like it is an entryway I could see for folks because it says nothing, means nothing, has no politics associated with it. So it's not scary. . . . Because you can be body positive and be dieting, according to half of these people."

A quick scroll through social media for #bodypositive finds fat people exercising, chubby (not fat) people talking about size acceptance, before/after weight loss pictures of people who are thin and thinner, and "buttocks compression garments." Even Adele chimed in on BoPo after the big reveal of her body post weight loss. In her "One Night Only" CBS special interview with Oprah, she says, "I was body positive then and I'm body positive now." She also told *British Vogue*, "You don't need to be overweight to be body positive, you can be any shape or size."[11] Which, as Shana noted, is one of the challenges with body positivity as the solution.

Now, even Lizzo herself sees the limits in the argument of body positivity as a solution. She says,

> I think it's lazy for me to just say I'm body positive at this point. It's easy. I would like to be body-normative. I want to normalize my body. And not just be like, "Ooh, look at this cool movement. Being fat is body positive." No, being fat is normal. I think now, I owe it to the people who started this to not just stop here. We have to make people uncomfortable again, so that we can continue to change. Change is always uncomfortable, right?[12]

Body positivity is not liberation.

chapter six

Can We Eat Our Way to Liberation?

HAVING A BODY IS INCONVENIENT.

Feeding a body is hard.

For most of us over the age of eighteen, feeding it involves choices, many choices, multiple times every day. It can be exhausting. It's easy to avoid it altogether.

While Lexi stayed with us during the COVID lockdown, she was working overnight shifts and going to school full-time. There were just a few hours during which we were all at home and awake. During her study breaks, sometimes we'd hear her door creak open and the dragging of feet across the floor. She'd appear in the kitchen and sigh. Next she would open the fridge door and begin shuffling food around only to close it just before the fridge's alarm went off to tell her the door had been open for too long. Following this, she'd lean over, open the freezer door, and begin rustling through its contents only to shut it as well. Next up were all the cupboards. Then it was back to the fridge. She was waiting for a meal to manifest itself, but it never did. Making decisions about what to eat and taking the time to cook required too much effort. She'd grab a glass, rest her head on the fridge door while she filled it up from the dispenser below, and then shuffle back to her room. When my spouse or I needed to grab something from the additional storage closet in her room, we'd oftentimes find things like a half-eaten box of white cheddar Cheez-Its wedged in the crack between the bed and the wall or next to her pillow. I'd mom her about it. "Cheez-Its, though delicious, are not a meal." She'd shrug and tell me that "it's better than not eating at all," which I always conceded was true. Feeding a body is hard.

. . .

PEOPLE OFTEN MAKE DIETITIAN APPOINTMENTS SEEKING OUT very specific food plans they can follow, down to the time of day, type of food, and amount. Some folks want this for weight loss, but in my experience most are just overworked, tired, and don't want to make any more decisions. And I get it. Outsourcing these choices seems like knowing how to use one's resources. Some dietitians, nutritionists, coaches, personal trainers, and social media influencers make a lot of money providing these plans; there's a large market for a plug-and-play program. In addition to the false promises of weight loss, I believe that many people seek out plans due to the comfort to be found in following the right way to eat, which specific meal plans and dieting provide.

For those looking to deviate from the rigidity and plans of dieting, there are the not-a-diet diets, or perhaps the anti-diets, that are billed as the ways to eat that don't have rules. In my practice I've found that the not-a-diets, like intuitive eating, have the same eating guardrails and can get tripped up in the same structure and safety that plug-and-play programs and dieting provide. If we're not eating with a goal of weight loss, frameworks like intuitive eating can still let us know when we're eating in the Right Way. They provide principles by which we can stay reassured. When I first heard of the framework, it was the perfect antidote to the calories in–calories out pyramid scheme I had been taught. And it was A Way to practice—until it wasn't.

• • •

I WAS INTRODUCED TO THE TEN PRINCIPLES OF INTUITIVE EATING in the early 2010s. On the surface, eating intuitively is revolutionary; there isn't a list of food, points, calories, macros, or anything to count, weigh, or measure. It was a huge relief. The book *Intuitive Eating: A Revolutionary Anti-Diet Approach*, written by two dietitians, was first published in 1996; its principles advocate eating what you truly want to eat. You're to "make peace with food" and "honor your hunger." It espouses giving oneself "unconditional permission to eat"—but only, ever, when you're hungry.

The "no rules" principles were a perfect landing spot after I realized that what is supposed to be unequivocally true about calories is anything but. For a few years I had some successes introducing clients to intuitive eating. It was a not-a-diet with the safety features of a diet; it still offered the road map to your destination of becoming "intuitive." I had a small private practice and hosted groups for people to learn more about intuitive eating and how to integrate it into their life. I wrote blogs about it and I talked with my clients about finding food freedom via intuitive eating.

But what I had thought to be revolutionary slowly revealed itself to be another way for my clients to overthink their food choices:

"I'm not always hungry on my lunch break. Should I still eat?"

"How full is full without being too full?"

"What if I'm satisfied but still hungry, or what if I'm full but not satisfied?"

"What is the perfect level of hunger I should aim for before eating?"

"So, if I'm out to lunch and want dessert but I'm not hungry anymore, should I skip it?"

"What if a friend asks me to dinner but I ate a late lunch, should I eat anything?"

"How do I go grocery shopping for the week when I don't know what I'm going to be truly hungry for the next day?"

I realized that what I was providing to my clients wasn't helping them achieve food freedom at all, and it was often causing more overthinking than a plug-and-play diet did. Also, WTF was food freedom anyhow? The final straw was when I saw how undernourished a variety of people became after adopting the idea that they should only eat when hungry.

When some people are stressed, depressed, or lacking in sleep, they might have decreased appetite. Some medications and some illnesses cause appetite changes. Sensory and cognitive differences can also lead to people not having a sense of hunger. People who have a history of food deprivation are typically not consistently hungry. In each of these circumstances, I have seen people become undernourished after thinking they shouldn't eat unless hungry. People were confused when I suggested eating when not hungry; they felt like they were doing something wrong. Others were able to justify dietary restriction after recognizing that the less often they ate, the less hungry they would become. I saw people get deeper into their eating disorders by only eating when their body would tell them to do so.

It turned out that intuitive eating was not for my clinical practice.

In 2020, I saw a marked uptick in articles and social media posts about intuitive eating and an increase in the number of people making dietitian appointments just wanting to hear more about intuitive eating. *Anti-Diet*, Christy Harrison's book, offered the framework of intuitive eating as the solution to dieting, and it was gaining steam again. Following the Ten Principles of Intuitive Eating seemed to be the new Right Way to eat food.

But I wanted to know, who were these solutions for?

. . .

"ANDROGYNY READS THIN AND WHITE." A FRIEND OF MINE connects their gender identity to their eating disorder development. They shared that when they were at their thinnest, and deepest in their eating disorder, they felt most affirmed because they were the closest they had been to "what nonbinary supposedly looks like" in our society. My friend could never be white, but they could be thinner. They stood a chance to be seen and celebrated in their nonbinary gender identity. Eating when they were hungry, or at least when their treatment team told them to do so, meant possibly giving that up.

A client of mine, Josh, recognized his connection between food and gender this way: "Turns out the problem with my belly and thighs is that there wasn't fur on them!"

. . .

"WELCOME BACK!" I TOLD JOSH WHEN HE SAT DOWN ON THE suede couch. "How have you been?" The on again, off again nature of COVID waves in 2021 meant that dietitian appointments weren't always in person. That day I was back in the office; it was great to see folks' faces again even if half was hidden by a mask.

Josh replied that he was cautiously optimistic that he was doing well in his eating disorder recovery. We'd started working together a couple of years prior, before his gender transition. He'd made his first dietitian appointment because "my therapist wanted me to meet with a dietitian just to be sure I'm eating enough." (You, Reader, will likely not be surprised that, no, he wasn't eating enough.) Josh was shocked at my assessment, and was angry about it. Later he told me that he'd been able to convince other dietitians that he was fine. "I had placed the plastic beans on the segmented plates, followed the charts of time on the x-axis and satiety on the y-axis that compared . . . carbs, fat, and protein. I impressed them with my in-depth knowledge of nutrition research and careful planning of vitamins." He told me that I "absolutely gutted" him with my feedback. But he scheduled a follow-up appointment and we continued to explore the functions that his eating patterns served.

At the beginning, Josh was vegan as a personal and political identity. Initially, Josh and I spent our fair share of moments negotiating whether hummus might be a condiment, side dish, or meal. Over time he recognized that being vegan was a good strategy for organizing his eating. Having a narrow list of foods to choose from made it easier to make choices and gave clear rules for which foods he could eat, which ones he should avoid, where to get food, and a reason for him to repeat the same foods over and over. Over time we also worked out that having a vegan diet was an easy way for him to decline invitations to restaurants and food-related gatherings, thus avoiding uncomfortable situations. He got to say no to food and to awkward conversations.

We realized that specific food recommendations, rather than listening to hunger cues, were helpful, so we worked on ways to be clear without counting or measuring. At one appointment he brought in his lunch container and I pulled my snack container out of my bag. They were equal in size.

When Josh started eating meals from meal containers, not snack containers, and became more flexible with the foods he ate, his body started to change. He'd expected some weight gain but hadn't anticipated the feelings of distress that resulted from weight gain in certain areas of his body. He hadn't expected to navigate gender dysphoria in addition to school, work, and maintaining relationships.

Josh and I did not talk about listening to his body. There was never a reason for me to introduce intuitive eating. The principles of: "Discover the satisfaction factor" and "Make peace with food" were irrelevant. We didn't talk about rejecting diet culture or the thin ideal; why would we? There was fear and uncertainty in the reality of eating food. Figuring out what was "intuitive" when eating didn't apply. The choice *to* eat was radical in and of itself. Instead of talking about feeling his fullness, we walked out into the waiting room to make a gender care medical appointment. We worked together on eating stability as he explored and then embraced his gender identity.

During our in-person check-in during COVID, he let me know that he was eating food and exercising for fun rather than for acute and urgent anxiety management; things were going well. We planned to have fewer visits that were further apart. Leaving the office that day was when he paused and said, "Turns out the problem with my belly and thighs is that there wasn't fur on them." We smiled and I laughed a bit. That was the best line about eating disorder recovery that I'd heard in a while. We acknowledged that receiving gender care wasn't the solution to his eating disorder, but he definitely wouldn't have progressed as far as he had without it.

A year later, Josh and I still haven't discussed intuitive eating. What for? One principle of the framework tells us to "challenge the food police" and, I gotta say, for many of us, the police in uniform and the systems that support them are far more threatening than those policing food. Those institutions are often the primary reasons some people change their eating patterns to conform their bodies to meet the demands of white supremacy. Josh and I talked about the safety to be found in passing as a cis person, not about listening to his body.

So, who was intuitive eating for?

● ● ●

TAMAR ADLER, A FORMER CHEF AND CONTRIBUTING EDITOR TO *Vogue* magazine, a fashion and beauty publication that has always "welcomed a certain type of employee—someone who is thin and white,"[1] found that intuitive eating was for her.

In February of 2020, Adler wrote a story for *Vogue* detailing her lunch with dietitian Elyse Resch, the cocreator of intuitive eating and its principles and steps and coauthor of, you guessed it, *Intuitive Eating*. Resch and Adler met for an interview over a meal at Wolfgang Puck's CUT—a restaurant at which you can spend more for a steak dinner than is provided for a month's groceries on government food assistance. Adler's fangirl energy and enthusiasm for the idea of a diet with no rules are palpable throughout the piece; she details Resch's dewy glow and flowy clothing, markers of both class and ease.

During this interview, Resch taught Adler three steps to making meal choices at restaurants.

"Step one in intuitive eating . . . start a meal with a healthy hunger. Don't eat a late lunch if you want to be excited for dinner, but don't be so hungry you demolish the breadbasket." Not too hungry, not too full; just the right amount of hunger. Adler noted that she was starving by the time this interview began. Oops.

Step two for Adler: "Clear my mind and read the menu closely, attuned to which dishes would bring me pleasure and satisfaction."

(These steps are different from rules, right?)

Step three: "Believe that all foods are morally equivalent. None is better or worse than another."

She marveled that "in the long term, following a program whose only rule is 'no rules' seems as low-stress as warm hydrotherapy."

In the same interview Adler and Resch discussed the steady increase in the popularity of intuitive eating over the last decade. While some folks pointed to *Anti-Diet* as a catalyst, Resch had a different theory. "It's Trump."[2] "After so many decades of being told to be thinner—which, [Resch] notes, coincided with women entering the workplace—women have had enough. 'Trump pushed us over the edge. We won't stand for being told how to look or sound or be anymore,'" Resch claimed. And "The overt misogyny of the current administration might, according to [Resch's] theory, spur actual liberation from restrictive eating."

Actual liberation. From the oppression of dieting. Here we are again, Susan. The kind of liberation that we can eat ourselves toward isn't the liberation I need.

Intuitive eating resonated with Adler, a thin white woman. It likely resonated for all readers of *Vogue*, a publication that "set a standard that has favored white, Eurocentric notions of beauty."[3]

Of course it did.

• • •

IN 2020, MOST OF MY COLLEAGUES WERE USING INTUITIVE EATING. I'm aware that I might just not be a good salesperson for the framework, so as it was becoming more mainstream I decided to try again; I'm always open to learning more. I sought out three of my colleagues, dietitians who had paid the thousands of dollars to become certified eating disorder specialists (each of whom was thin and white, because, well, statistics), to tell me more about how they talk about intuitive eating with their clients. I asked each how they describe intuitive eating to their clients and how their clients will know whether they're eating intuitively.

Their answers were identical.

All three crossed their hands over their chest and fluttered them a bit, looking like the wings of a monarch butterfly had sprung from their collarbones. They told me that intuitive eating feels like that.

All three, without being influenced by the others.

Feels like what? They couldn't tell me what intuitive eating meant in words. One said that the International Association of Eating Disorders Professionals Foundation (iaedp), the org that certifies eating disorder therapists and promotes intuitive eating in the curriculum, didn't really talk about intuitive eating in the certification materials, that the assumption was "when you're doing it you'll know." Ummmm, will I?

Following these confusing conversations, I sought out a webinar from an intuitive eating dietitian. I was curious whether, years after my introduction, the authors and disciples of *Intuitive Eating* had figured out a way to be less rigid, less prescriptive, and less confusing than they had been in years past.

I logged on from my kitchen table to hear "If you're not eating for physical reasons, know that you're doing the best you can with the tools you have." Womp. The dietitian opened his talk about how to heal one's relationship with food via eating intuitively with this line. What might read to some as a gentle approach continues to enforce that eating only for physical reasons is the Right Way.

The dietitian shared that "Intuitive Eaters Do 4 Things": (1) have unconditional permission to eat; (2) eat for physical rather than emotional reasons; (3) rely on internal hunger and fullness cues to determine how much to eat; and (4) have body–food congruence, which includes "interoceptive awareness."

The middle two were consistent with the primary hang-ups and concerns of most of my clients—we're supposed to eat food, not too much, and only for biological reasons. And somehow this is supposed to make feeding ourselves easier. I just couldn't see how.

I returned to my day job the following Monday and was asked about the conference by my then team. I shared that the synopsis of intuitive eating continues to be that we should only be eating for biological reasons and only however much is necessary. That from time to time, we might slip up and eat for pleasure, but we shouldn't be hard on ourselves; we're doing the best we can when faced with temptation.

Sound familiar?

My then boss likened this to the idea of having sex only for procreation. Oop! The abstinence-only messages in my middle school sex ed classes that Mrs. Jaimeson espoused seemed very similar to what the disciples of intuitive eating are telling us about food today. The idea that our body is a biological organism that has needs for functional purposes only is similar to the idea that sex is only for fertilizing an egg and should be used for nothing more. We're to avoid experiencing joy and pleasure with eating and with sex; both can lead us down a dark path.

Such a mandate to avoid pleasure takes us back to the associations of hedonism with both Blackness and fatness that were written centuries ago. The religiosity of intuitive eating, which I had been caught up in myself at one time, continues today. And the message to avoid eating for anything other than biology was

the primary sticking point for me with intuitive eating all along—
the problematizing and pathologizing of eating food when not
biologically hungry.

The book *Intuitive Eating* finally changed its seventh principle
from "Cope with Your Emotions Without Food" to "Cope with
Your Emotions with Kindness" in its fourth edition, published in
2020. What I thought could be a change in philosophy was pretty
much word for word the former edition, including "eating for an
emotional hunger may only make you feel worse in the long run."
This is consistent with the philosophies of the diet industry and
those who value things like "willpower" and being a tightly regu-
lated person overall. It is a gentler way of pathologizing things that
are neutral, like eating for celebrations, while grieving, while hanging out with friends, with your friend who is struggling, because
you failed an exam, because it's Wednesday, or Thursday, or any day,
and it tastes good. It's literally fine.

The authors further patronize people who eat when they aren't
hungry and call them "disconnected eaters" who may block their
"ability to detect [their] intuitive signals."[4] One of the authors detailed the freedom she found when she finally allowed herself to go
out to restaurants with friends and drink water while everyone else
was eating their food. This is Eating Disorder 101, and also a way to
stop getting dinner invitations. If I was going to share a pitcher of
water with someone, I'd probably just call them on my commute
home from work rather than ask them to dinner. I tell my clients
that if a friend calls them for support after something like a breakup
and asks to get takeout or get ice cream, I don't want the first thing
they think of to be "Now, am I hungry?" or "What am I craving?"
or "Should I eat again? I had dinner a couple hours ago." I want

them to calculate how long it will take them to arrive and support their friend in the way that friend has asked to be supported, to just eat the food and let it be a typical Tuesday evening, nothing more, nothing less.

Additionally, many people are "disconnected eaters." And that's fine. Eating when supposedly disconnected for those who don't get consistent hunger cues is a way for them to simply Eat Food.

Those who may not have regular access to food need to eat in a way that allows them to eat more when food is available. It's a privilege to eat only when hungry and to stop when feeling just the right amount of fullness. With 10.5 percent of American households experiencing food insecurity, and 5.1 million households experiencing very low food security in 2020, "disconnected eating" should never be pathologized.[5] Fifty-one percent of students participate in the National School Lunch Program, receiving free and reduced-price lunches and sometimes breakfasts. Though the experiences of children in these programs differ, school meals may come with a scoop of mixed vegetables and shame.[6] Rather than experiencing the stigma society applies to families who receive financial assistance, some students decide to skip the meal altogether.

I once had a client who was in vet school and working from five a.m. to ten p.m. She presented with binge eating concerns because she would come home at night and eat an entire pizza. From what she'd been told, this was the wrong way to eat pizza and she was convinced she had binge eating disorder. It turned out that ten p.m. was the only time during the day she got to eat food at all. If she was hungry during her shift, she had to ignore it because the students weren't allowed breaks during the day. She also needed to finish her chart notes while she was eating at night—she was a "disconnected eater." She was fine.

For whom is eating actually intuitive?

• • •

An underlying thread of intuitive eating is that the Right Way is to Eat Less.

If we give ourselves unconditional permission to eat, the theory is that we will eat less because we won't feel like food is scarce.

If we intuitively feel our fullness, we won't eat as much.

If we make peace with certain foods, we just won't eat as much of them.

If we "discover the satisfaction factor," per the intuitive eating principles, we will eat less.

In the midst of my writing this chapter, a colleague of mine sent me an Instagram Reel of a dietitian who uses intuitive eating with her clients. She begins the video by eating a slice of deep-dish pizza, melted cheese strings stretching from her mouth, with the caption "When someone thinks they'll only eat 'unhealthy' as an intuitive eater . . ." The video then goes on to show photos of picture-perfect foods, like a whole-grain wrap, a "veggie-packed" chicken shawarma salad, and a yogurt and granola "banana split," with the dietitian stating: "I CAN eat pizza all day 🍕 . . . but I don't want to" and "I get why people think intuitive eating is just eating 'unhealthy' and not caring about nutrition or health."[7] According to this dietitian and many like her, even the diets that let you "eat whatever you want" aren't supposed to result in us actually eating whatever we want. It still needs to look a certain way; it's not supposed to be pizza all day.

Christy Harrison agrees. One of the myths of intuitive eating she busted in a 2020 article in *Self* magazine was that "intuitive eating means only eating cake and cheeseburgers for the rest of your life."

Statements like these, like eating only for procreation—oops, I mean for biological reasons!—though perhaps well intended, inherently reinforce the idea that there are still ways we should eat and ways we should not. They are phrased differently from the typical dieting messages: *You should not eat too much cake, fries, or too many cheeseburgers*, but the impact is the same.

With intuitive eating, we're supposed to eat less, and it's supposed to look a certain way.

What is supposed to bring "liberation" provides the same outcomes as both dieting and the messages about how we should eat to be Good People. Morality is tied to both eating emotionally and body size, as people connect fatness with not keeping one's "appetite in check." We assume someone performing restraint and abstaining from emotional eating is one who has self-control. Self-control, when only eating for biological reasons, is still something that Good People have.

In 2020, I saw for the first time eating disorder clinicians and intuitive eating providers finally give their clients and the public permission to gain five pounds, because, as they told us, if that was the worst thing that happened to us during a pandemic, it meant we didn't die. The same clinicians were all of a sudden providing their endorsement of emotional eating, but only because we were struggling to cope with collective grief and a global shutdown.

Apparently, only when the alternative is death will we publicly talk about it being fine to gain weight (but only five pounds) and eat when we aren't biologically hungry.

. . .

IN SOME CIRCLES, PERFORMING INTUITIVE EATING OFFERS FAT respectability. A friend of mine shared that when she came across the book *Intuitive Eating*, which discusses the Health benefits of intuitive eating, she took the concept to the doctor's office as proof that she was eating in the Right Way as a fat person. She quickly realized medical providers had no idea what intuitive eating was. Intuitive eating also provides a justification ("it's intuitive") for eating ice cream in public rather than just because it is a friend's birthday or simply a Monday. It attempts to distance fat people from the hedonism assigned; it's okay to eat a donut as long as it's intuitive. Another friend of mine notes that eating food because it tastes good is problematized for fat folks like her, but if you're thin, society just labels you a foodie for your "disconnected eating."

. . .

I MET MY CLIENT SOPHIA WHILE WORKING AT UC DAVIS.

After calling her back from the waiting area, I welcomed her into the office. She had a seat on the couch.

"How can I help you today?" I asked.

Sophia told me she'd made the appointment because she was interested in learning more about intuitive eating. She had been looking for how and what to eat after having moved to Davis and needing to make meals on her own. She'd been looking for resources on social media and found intuitive eating influencers talking about the best new way to eat.

"I'm not looking to lose weight or anything, I'm just trying to figure out what to eat on my own," she told me.

"What kinds of foods did you eat while you were living at home?" I inquired.

"Oh, mostly Mexican food. My mom is Mexican and my dad is Black," she told me.

The intake paperwork I used at my university job requested that the incoming client write down the food they had eaten in the last three days. Hers had a lot of tofu, greens, whole grains, cauliflower "rice," and vegan meats.

I asked her about the shift in eating patterns and how she felt about the foods she grew up eating.

"But aren't tacos unhealthy?" she replied.

Oh, Davis. One could insert foods like enchiladas, white rice, noodles, pasta, and many other culturally relevant foods in place of tacos for foods that are labeled "unhealthy." I'd had this conversation many times. Davis's food culture is very, well, white. Sophia had white housemates, also in her environmental science major, who would regularly discuss food and even make comments when Sophia would eat white rice instead of brown rice. Sophia had taken a sustainable agriculture class and was given the impression that she shouldn't be eating certain foods that she enjoyed.

She'd made the appointment because she just wasn't sure what or how to eat anymore. She had been able to feel less vigilant in her house by conforming to the food respectability norms but wasn't ever happy about what she was eating, and she felt distant from her culture.

We talked about the safety found in conforming to norms of a situation. I told her that I understood. We talked about her interest in intuitive eating as a way to improve her relationship with food. Instead of walking her through the principles, we discussed the ways that the narratives of colonization have impacted which foods are considered good or bad by Western society. We discussed what that meant for her and the reality that conforming is often easier. I connected her with student centers on campus and other resources so she could connect with people and have conversations about her Mexican heritage and share food.

I don't pretend that food has no moral value with my clients, because it does. How we eat, what we eat, and where we shop are indicators of our willingness to perform for whiteness. I don't try to convince my clients to eat what they truly crave if they find social and/or emotional safety assimilating into the norms of their city or school setting. Our food choices are, indeed, tied to morality and our body size is tied to our virtue. People can find community and mitigate some harm with food respectability. Assimilation into the colonialist culture provides safety if one's cultural foods are pathologized. Discarding one's traditional dishes in favor of arugula and amaranth offers proof to those around them that they know how to follow the rules, even though their bodies may not. We leave people even more impacted and without agency and efficacy when we ignore their experiences. We literally whitewash their narrative. We see, again, individual solutions to societal problems that benefit those who already have privilege. Those who benefit from the newest way to eat do; the rest of us are left thinking we're just doing it wrong.

chapter seven

Health Is Killing Us

EVERY ONE OF MY BLACK FRIENDS HAS A CHRONIC ILLNESS. We share updates on our health and strategies for illness management.

We check in about medical appointments.

We share how we've advocated for the care we need.

We remind each other to take our vitamin D.

We support each other and provide community care.

We cry.

The commonality here is Blackness.

It would be easy to argue that Blackness is what makes us sick.

Some people do.

They're not wrong.

. . .

"HEALTH DISPARITIES, ESPECIALLY MEDICAL RACISM, IS TOO controversial," she told us. I had been invited to speak during a plenary session about health disparities at the 2022 Healthy Kitchens, Healthy Lives (HKHL) conference. After I shared my potential talking points, this was how one of the other speakers responded; I'll call her Sheila. Sheila is a non-Black physician and was invited to speak during the same plenary. After hearing what I planned to say, she simply dropped out rather than be associated with my work.

Too controversial.

Upon hearing her assessment, I remember squinting at her Zoom box, trying to read her face for sarcasm; I must have been missing something. I asked about her specific concerns. She said that her hesitance was particular to the HKHL audience and organizers, less so about the topic overall. What I was planning to say likely wouldn't be received well.

Instead of joining me in talking about health disparities in the plenary, she stuck to making a separate presentation about legumes, whole grains, and leafy greens. She chose to stay safe. Leveraging her positionality to have hard conversations was apparently too great a risk. At the time, I didn't understand how health disparities, something with arguably more conclusive research than nutrition—a topic with much contradictory evidence—could be up for debate. Nor why a person of color would choose to align themselves with a community that couldn't talk about medical racism.

You might be wondering how I had been asked to the conference in the first place. A fair inquiry; it's something I continue to question myself. HKHL is a partnership of the Culinary Institute of America and the Harvard T. H. Chan School of Public Health. It is an annual gathering of healthcare providers and executives, along with food service directors and chefs who come to Napa, California, from across the world to learn from a faculty curated by Dr. David Eisenberg, the director of culinary nutrition at Harvard. The event was virtual in 2021, and per the events of 2020, the conference needed to address health disparities in its return to in-person gathering in 2022. To be on brand with corporate and academic commitments to diversity, they also needed at least one Black person to speak.

Cue me. Only me.

During initial calls with organizers and speakers, I learned the Culinary Institute and Harvard's simple two-step solution to everything that ails us: eat less and move more. Yawn. Upon hearing about the group's philosophy and how they frame both Health and eating, I offered the organizers an opportunity to uninvite me. I tried—multiple times—to convince them that I wouldn't be able to back up their ideas about Health. I won't preach that all people need to have a Eurocentric diet, one filled with brown rice and olive oil. I'm just not the best fit.

Health disparities are not solved by teaching people how to cook quinoa and put sliced almonds on salads. Historical inequities will not be solved with eating more fiber and buying a Peloton bike. The positioning of individual solutions to societal problems lets disparities persist. These individual solutions enable us to blame people for being unwell rather than addressing the structures that contribute to well-being. The topic of health disparities was clearly an afterthought to the conference. When I asked about this, the HKHL organizers told me that they have to start somewhere, and this plenary was a good intro for the conference attendees. I shared that post-2020 they may be interested in the *idea* of my work, but not in the truths that I tell. And that's okay, it's not personal. I told them that they could easily find a Black dietitian who shared their values because all of us had been trained to tell people to stop eating white rice. And multiple times the organizers told me that my philosophy and approach to patient care were what the faculty and participants need to hear, even if they weren't ready to hear it. I'm ever curious and enjoy a good awkward moment, so I agreed. What was the worst that could happen?

Only two other speakers, both dietitians, remained willing to talk about health disparities in the plenary session. We started drafts of our presentation slides and met via Zoom to discuss our progress. As we continued in the planning process, we were told that our presentation needed to be approved by someone named Walter before we would be approved. I was told that this Walter fellow is the "grandfather of nutrition" and enjoys sharing that he's married to a Black woman. Later into the process, I finally took to the interwebs and found that Walter is Dr. Walter Willett, a professor of epidemiology and nutrition at the Harvard T. H. Chan School of Public Health and professor of medicine at Harvard Medical School. He was chair of the Harvard School of Public Health Department of Nutrition for twenty-five years. It's quite an esteemed career. Willett is cocreator and headliner of the HKHL conference, which relies heavily on his personal scholarship as The Path forward for the nutrition, culinary, and medical fields. The gathering is essentially an opportunity to pay homage to him and network among his disciples. On the surface, it made sense that he would need to review our slides. We would need to be on brand with his message.

After preliminary research, I understood why anyone affiliated with the conference would think it was risky to talk about health disparities. Dr. Katherine Flegal, a former senior research scientist and distinguished consultant of the National Center for Health Statistics of the Centers for Disease Control and Prevention and consulting professor at the Stanford Prevention Research Center, documented the lengths Willett and Dr. Frank Hu, the current chair of the Department of Nutrition at the Harvard T. H. Chan School of Public Health, went to intimidate her and criticize her and her work. Flegal's research showed that "overweight" people live longer than those with a "normal/healthy weight," a conclusion in direct opposition to Willett's findings.

Flegal's treatment by Willett and Hu would certainly make people think twice about saying something that may bring the wrath of disputed Harvard researchers.[1]

When I shared my concerns about Willett with the HKHL organizer, I was told, flat out, that they wouldn't intervene or defend my work if Willett came after my career as well. Of course not. Protecting whiteness and power in institutions, while viewing all others as disposable, is central to this country's foundations and has trickled down into medicine. Pledging allegiance to those with institutional power and protecting them, even after new information shows one should behave otherwise, is how health disparities are created in the first place.[2] Reinforcing the centrality of whiteness and power in Health is required to maintain the status quo. And funding.

. . .

Health has been connected to whiteness for over a century, it's nothing new. Charles Davenport (1866–1944) was an advocate for (racial) Health. He was a Harvard-educated biologist and eugenicist invested in the concept of "better breeding" to save the white race from extinction. He believed that by keeping the bloodline in a superior state of Health, people assigned whiteness would increase their longevity while the "inferior races" would die off and that "if there be a serious support of research in eugenics and a willingness to be guided by clearly established facts in this field, the end of our species may long be postponed and the race may be brought to higher levels of racial health, happiness and effectiveness."[3] Davenport makes clear the moral imperative of white people to achieve higher levels of Health and connects the concepts to the structures of white supremacy.

John Harvey Kellogg (1852–1943), a doctor, nutrition evangelist, and businessman, more famous for his flakes of corn than for his legacy of eugenics, published an article in 1914 titled "Relation of Public Health to Race Degeneracy" in the *American Journal of Public Health*. With gains made in proper sanitation doctors of the time were able to focus on the larger issues impacting the white race. He stated, "There has been going on . . . a remarkable depreciation in racial vitality and stamina. The human race, or at least the civilized portion of it, is degenerating at a rapid rate."[4] There was a social imperative to achieve Health in the 1900s and the connection of Health to morality. Good (white, in this case) people pursued Health as their duty, to be loyal members of their race. We saw it in women's magazines in the 1900s and we see it today in the comradery and communities for those invested in restriction, constraint, and exercise in ways that promise thin, lean bodies and glowing Health.

• • •

THE CONFERENCE GAVE ME JORDAN PEELE *GET OUT* VIBES FROM the beginning. After arriving at the conference hotel in Napa, California, the evening prior to the first conference day, I dropped my bags in my room, unpacked a few things, and returned to the lobby to meet one of the two people who would join me on the panel. Before we could finish greeting each other, we were interrupted by a physician I'll call Tammy. I don't excel at small talk, so when I introduced myself, I said, "Hi, I'm Jessica Wilson. I'm speaking about racism and fatphobia in medicine; what are your experiences addressing this?" Tammy was initially quiet and contemplative and then asked me at least ninety-seven consultation questions over the next three days that started with phrases like, "But 'obesity' . . ." and "But don't you think we should tell people to lose weight when . . ." Though Tammy may have come from a place of curiosity, she was also enjoying an opportunity to spar with one of the few Black women there. We went back and forth discussing people's behaviors, access, weight, eating disorders, and valuing patients' humanity and autonomy. I used it as an opportunity to distill my experience into sentences rather than paragraphs as Tammy introduced me to at least ten people and started off each intro with, "This is Jessica, she thinks we shouldn't tell our patients they need to lose weight." She tried to disguise the fact that she was parading me around the conference like a spectacle, a sideshow: "Oh, here's someone else you should meet!" My cheeks were tired from the fake smile I kept plastered across my face. That first evening, while enjoying my fish tacos in silence, I sent my friend a quick Marco Polo video in which I told her there were "two doctors in hot pursuit of me" and laughed at myself and the situation. "I'm going to examine that part of my life."

The morning of the first conference day, I woke up fully alert at four a.m. Yikes. The free breakfast wasn't until eight a.m. and I was very grateful for my yesterday-self who had run across the street from my office to the Trader Joe's for snacks. After entertaining myself for hours, and realizing how comfortable having more than eighteen minutes to get ready in the morning could be, I set myself up in front of the mirror. When I reached into my toiletry case, my hand skipped right over my "natural" deodorant and right to the Secret antiperspirant I had acquired for just this occasion; I was ready. The Culinary Institute of America building is perhaps a quarter mile from the hotel. I spent the entire walk along the river bend cursing Lexi, who had taken me shopping over the winter holidays and encouraged me to "get with the times" and buy a pair of Chelsea boots. I'd chosen to wear them today, absolutely unprepared for how differently these boots fit compared to my 24/7 Chacos.

The Culinary Institute is a beautiful, multifloored complex with big floor-to-ceiling windows looking out over a bend in the Napa River. I arrived by myself and got in a good amount of people watching until I'd made it through registration. I was surprised that in my suit pants and sweater I was one of the most formally dressed individuals there, a first. I immediately missed my Chacos and jeggings.

We were surrounded by the values of restraint at the conference. The muffins were two bites' worth of food, as were the 1.5-inch-square pieces of frittata. We used saucer-sized plates; it gave strong tea party energy. The teacup with the spoon swirling from *Get Out* was all I could think about. Things were austere, refined. The meals were simply nibbles and noshes. With such small plates, I absolutely went back for breakfast seconds and perhaps thirds. I couldn't help but wonder if those who found me hypervisible, rather than invisible, were confirmed in their potential assignment of gluttony to my Blackness as I returned to the buffet line.

Health and its sister-wife, virtue, were ever present at the conference and offered us all an opportunity to perform Health if we didn't already have it. We could mingle and practice discussing how satisfying a two-ounce serving of oat milk vanilla frozen nondairy dessert with vegan brownie crumbles could be; who needed more? We got the opportunity to pretend that being offered a miniscone was better than eating one from a traditional bakery. I got to pretend that I enjoyed quinoa and kale more than I enjoyed the fish tacos and fries that I ate for three of the four dinners I was there because (1) they were delicious and (2) I don't like making choices when I'm emotionally spent—though I did switch between sweet potato fries and garlic fries—I'm not a monster!

• • •

A BODY IS SUPPOSED TO BE HEALTHY AT ALL TIMES. OUR BODIES, per their appearance, more than constitution, are assigned Health or un-Health. The expectations are clear and simple. Visual assessments for Health include ability, agility, thinness, binary gender presentation, heteronormativity, youth, middle- and upper-class clothing, and, ultimately, whiteness. Other observable signifiers include what we eat, where we shop for groceries, and whether/how we are physically active. We're to take care of our Health as if it were an inanimate object, something precious, fragile, and in need of constant tending. If we have not been assigned Health, we are to do everything in our power to achieve such a state, and if it's impossible for us to do so, we're to perform Health whenever possible. We're taught to value what Health looks like and shame others and ourselves if we don't conform.

When basic network television was our primary form of viewing at-home entertainment, television news would air stories about un-Healthy people that showed fat people out on the town with their heads cut out of the frame. Families sat down together to shame contestants on *The Biggest Loser*. I watched the fatphobia, racism, and classism of *Super Size Me* unfold in the theater with my friends. These activities, as well as public health's messages of fat panic and language like "epidemic," connected a lack of Health to fatness and inherently stigmatized both. In the aughts and early 2010s, my clients, those raised watching this programming, were very invested in a goal of Health, which was presented as a more altruistic reason to shrink their bodies compared to simply wanting to be skinny. Clients claimed to not care about what they weighed as long as they were Healthy. Many of my clients had developed disordered eating patterns to achieve Health, especially those whose parents had been caught up in the dichotomies of Healthy and un-Healthy food at the time. People like Jillian Michaels, her coconspirators, and those capitalizing on the idea that fatness is contagious made it impossible to untangle thinness from Health. Bullying with the intent to "motivate" people to become Healthy, as determined by thinness and "fitness," became commonplace and reinforced the idea that those who don't have Health were making the choice to be un-Healthy and are not worthy of humanity.

Health is yet another benchmark we have artificially constructed in the United States that Good People should achieve. In

1980, Robert Crawford discussed this in his article "Healthism and the Medicalization of Everyday Life." He notes that the United States had been "elevating health to a super value, a metaphor for all that is good in life" exemplified in the popularization of running and other fitness endeavors at the time. More than forty years later, Healthism continues to be something that we internalize for ourselves, we judge others by, and companies have found to be a valuable marketing hook. We can buy anything, from a ColonBroom "cleanse" to "ancient grains" and books and products to help us intermittently fast (hot take: everyone who is already skipping breakfast or doesn't have enough money for it—the majority of people in my experience—is already fasting. Are they Healthier?), all with the goal of achieving Health. Crawford also notes, "Healthism is a kind of elitist moralizing" in the context of blaming individuals for their own actions.[6]

I sent another Marco Polo video to the same friend during the morning break on day two of HKHL. Replaying it, months later, I noticed how exhausted and confused I was. Leaning on the balcony and staring at the river, I had many nonverbal pauses as I processed my experience. "I thought it was going to be differently morally intense, like weight loss, like we are eating healthy for weight loss and disease [prevention]."

"I'm wrong," I told her in the video. "The overt fatphobia has not been as strong as Healthism, which was surprising." I looked off to my right, my black KN95 mask hanging from my right ear. I told her it feels like "morality and abstention to justify my very expensive tastes, to justify why I only have Healthy friends, to justify my [elitism]."

"I'm at the Church of Healthy Kitchens" and it's "the religion of . . ." I paused, furrowed my brow, and tried to name it. "The religion of small plates???" I hadn't put my finger on it yet. I thanked her for listening to everything that was swirling inside my brain and went back into the building. I didn't want to miss the mindful eating talk, during which I learned that research participants had been told to chew their food forty times before swallowing, all in the name of mindfulness. Wow. I'm not sure chewing each bite forty times is what those who brought mindfulness to the Western world had hoped the practice would provide.

To make the connection between the quest for Health and elitism through food more clear, Harriet A. Washington's 2006 book *Medical Apartheid: The Dark History of Medical Experimentation on Black Americans from Colonial Times to the Present* quoted Robert J. Blendon, emeritus faculty at Harvard, saying, "What the French see in wine, Americans see in health." Washington goes on to say that "Americans consider access to excellent health—and even the most expensive means of maintaining it—their birthright. Americans enjoy ever-burgeoning longevity, extravagant nutrition, and everyday access to superb medical care, including expensive high-technology interventions."[7] At HKHL in Napa, we could get both: wine and Health. We got a literal taste of what the upper crust of society pays people to cook for them on a daily basis. There was a very clear Us vs. Those People flavor to the experience.

• • •

"ALL OF A SUDDEN I JUST NEEDED HEALTHY FOOD," SHE TOLD ME. I was talking to a Black therapist who had reached out for a Zoom coffee date. She wanted to know more about my work and explore referring clients to me as she transitioned her practice in a more "holistic Health" direction. During conversations like these, I engage and listen, and then I am up front about my philosophy and who I center in my work. I like to make clear that my primary interests lie in helping people Eat Food, not integrate goji berries, blue-green algae, and organic produce into their lives. The therapist agreed with what I had shared and then went on to tell me a story that she thought demonstrated her similar values. She told me that she had recently returned to her home state of Alabama for a family emergency, and the stress of being at her relative's hospital bedside made her urgently crave healthy food. She lamented how many fast-food restaurants there were in the state and all of the unhealthy food that people, including her family, were eating.

"So my aunt took me to a grocery store and I put fresh broccoli, tofu, brown rice, and some other foods in my basket. When I'd finished shopping she asked me, 'Have you gotten all of your bougie food yet?'" The therapist paused for my response; I had none. "And then we were in the checkout line and she pointed to my fresh broccoli and asked me why I didn't get the frozen broccoli because it's already cut and you could just pop it into the microwave!" she tells me. The therapist looked at me aghast and as if I, too, would be mirroring her despair about her aunt's comments. The therapist told me that she needed the superior nutrition of fresh vegetables, not frozen.*

Instead of mirroring the distress, I asked, "Why do you think your aunt would call your grocery items bougie?" And whether the ther-

---

* Frozen and fresh vegetables have comparable nutrition. Frozen veggies are flash frozen on site, whereas fresh produce is often shipped and can lose nutrients to light, heat, and air in the process.

apist had said anything about her choices that would lead to her aunt's response. She looked at me with some confusion-surprise and said, "I had never thought about how she felt in that moment, I'd only ever reflected on how I felt." Even those we assume to be the most self-aware can get caught up in moralizing food choices and judging others who don't align. This therapist was putting distance between herself and her family; *those people* who didn't eat fresh broccoli versus herself, who was making the Healthy choices. Health is fresh, not frozen. Health is whichever food spoils more quickly. Health is always the more expensive choice. Health is a value of US society, and those of us who will always be in the lowest caste may gain closer proximity to whiteness by performing Health and reinforcing its value among others.

Today, those who don't conform to expectations of Health crafted by whiteness are easily discarded by society and, frankly, dismissed by the medical-industrial complex. The structures of Healthism and ableism value those who look and behave in the Right Ways. Because society upholds the language of "healthy behaviors" and inherently treats those who engage in such—*and* those who simply look like they do—better than others, there can be much gained in the performance of Health. We can conform to what Health demands by putting distance between us and those who don't perform; we can engage in Health respectability.

• • •

WHILE AT THE CONFERENCE, I COULDN'T HELP BUT WONDER WHO the solution to all that ails us ("eat less, move more") was for. The obvious answer was that it was for those who could afford the $1,500 conference fee, travel to/from, and the hundreds of dollars per night lodging in Napa. But was it also for the farmworkers picking grapes and tending to the land who are moving all day, every day? Was it for the nearly 2,640 food-insecure kids in Napa County who lived in food-insecure households in 2019? I'll never know because the conference never mentioned them. And it didn't seem out of place.

The entire conference was focused on the foods people need to *choose* in order to be Healthy. The messages from HKHL resembled the individualism and neoliberalism found in many food policies.[8] Focusing on individual choices as the primary proxy for Health and the primary contributor to how much someone will weigh offers the opportunity to create economies and policies that keep "healthy" foods expensive and only available in certain areas. Policies and the researchers who influence them are able to keep "unhealthy foods" entirely associated with Black and Brown communities and individuals. Focusing on choice assumes people have choices to make in the first place. The expectation that someone take two buses to get to a grocery store across the city to spend six dollars on an avocado instead of getting a single stick of butter for a dollar from the corner store is consistent with the *pull yourself up by your bootstraps* mentality that permeates this country. Not only is it unrealistic, it isn't going to help anyone. This narrative disregards the impacts of redlining, zoning codes, lending practices, and the intention with which certain communities have been denied the development of grocery stores that contribute to food apartheid.[9] Instead of food deserts, which imply a landscape that is naturally occurring, food apartheid acknowledges that the food environments in primarily Black and Brown communities are by design.

Having a conference in Napa, California, a destination known for its wine and its pretentiousness, is brilliant. It is a subtle way to skew the audience toward those who can afford to shop at Whole Foods or a local co-op and who believe if we teach poor people how to cook with brassicas and bulgur that everyone can be healthy and happy. It appeals to the saviorism and paternalism of messaging like "if they only knew."[10] This scapegoats any need for the conference to address structural and systemic causes of poverty, and it didn't. It didn't seem like a lapse in planning. There really was no need to discuss something that couldn't fit within the narrow boundaries of Health defined by the conference. And they didn't.

During one of the last plenary sessions on day one of the conference, there was a presentation about how to make southern food healthy again by the white chef and dietitian who would join me on the panel. He was addressing a question from a doctor in the audience who asked how to make her patients in poverty eat whole grains and vegetables. In his answer the dietitian introduced the term *food apartheid* to the audience and was interrupted by David Eisenberg chuckling into the microphone. My jaw dropped to the floor and the flurry of texts I sent in all caps to friends and colleagues was unprecedented. Get. Out.

The next morning Eisenberg and I got on the hotel elevator together heading to the lobby and I took those seventeen seconds during which we were trapped in the same tight space to ask about his familiarity with the concept. He told me that he'd never heard the term *food apartheid* before that Q and A. "Is it new?" he asked. I said that it was newer than the term *food desert*, and it has been in popular publications; he could google it. There was no need for him to know about food apartheid in his line of work; folks who live in areas with food apartheid don't often get to make *healthy choices*, even if they have cooking skills.

It wasn't just food. There was also no need for the conference to address the other factors that contribute to Health, or the lack thereof. During one plenary, two speakers, a white dietitian and Tammy, were asked for their views on the connection between trauma and body weight. Tammy said some form of a word salad that didn't address the question and showed no understanding of the intersection between the two, followed by the dietitian who said, yes, some people experience trauma. She recommends her patients talk to a therapist who can address the trauma so the two of them can get back to working on weight loss. The end.

* * *

WHEN FRESH, IFASINA, SHANA, AND I JOINED OUR CALL TO TALK about respectability and body positivity, and after realizing it had been six years since we'd all been in the same place at the same time, our dialogue naturally shifted to life updates, which inherently included our health and medical appointments. At that time I was a couple months out from my medical leave from work. I was considering the pros and cons of getting brain surgery to eliminate or at least reduce my seizures after the recent caucacity-induced flare. I was also at a loss for how to address some new seizure symptoms that had stumped my neurologist. Each of us on the call was navigating new diagnoses. We traded horror stories and absurd encounters with medical professionals, and what was going well. We discussed how we navigate the healthcare system overall and lamented that even some Black medical providers can get caught up in the white supremacy and power dynamics of medicine. We didn't discuss our health, or lack thereof, as a value or a moral failing. It was just a part of our updates, the natural flow of the conversation, an opportunity to witness and show care for each other. What we knew to be the unspoken truth was that we will never be healthy.

Black women are diagnosed just for existing. Steatopygia, from the Greek *steato* meaning "fat" and *pygia* meaning "buttocks," is defined as "excessive fat of the buttocks, usually seen in women and sometimes called Hottentot Bustle," so called because Sarah Baartman was considered a Hottentot, the name given to her and the Khoikhoi people by Dutch colonists.[11] This affliction is characterized by "protrusion and excessive fatness of just the buttocks region." What a friend of mine lovingly calls her butt shelf and what many women pay thousands of dollars to augment has a current diagnosis code of E65 for localized adiposity.

In *Medical Apartheid*, Harriet Washington presents Samuel A. Cartright, a doctor in Louisiana in the mid-1800s who invented diseases and assigned them to Blackness. The "principal symptoms" of these diseases "seemed to be a lack of enthusiasm for slavery. Escape might have seemed like normal behavior for a slave in ancient Greece or Rome, but Cartright medically condemned such behavior in American blacks, offering a diagnosis of drapetomania, from the Greek words for flight and insanity."[12] Thus making the desire for physical and emotional safety as a Black person a disease.

Medicine and public health remain invested in defining health in ways that Black women will never fit if the current narrative persists. Blackness was to never be healthy because the white race is Health. Da'Shaun L. Harrison, in their book *Belly of the Beast: The Politics of Anti-Fatness as Anti-Blackness*, takes this argument further:

"Medical apartheid . . . is foundational to the creation of race—which is the creation of the Black which is the creation of the Slave. For as long as there is a Black there is a subject to be experimented on; for as long as there is a subject to be experimented on, health will always already be inaccessible to the Slave. And as this is the case, health is a framework in which no Black person can ever fit."[13] Black people may gain proximity to whiteness should we perform Health to the greatest extent possible, but we'll never be healthy in the end.

• • •

THE ERASURE AND MINIMIZATION OF THE EXPERIENCES OF ANYONE who doesn't have Health are predictable.

Black women have been essential to the development of modern medicine, all while never getting the medical care reserved for our white peers. The mutilation and torture of enslaved Black women are at the foundation of our current obstetrics and gynecological medicine understandings and have contributed to the narrative that Black women don't feel pain. The pregnancy-related mortality rate for Black women with at least a college degree was five times as high as that of white women with a similar education for the ten years between 2007 and 2016, and Black infants were twice as likely to die compared to non-Hispanic white infants.

Looking at this information, one could make the argument, again, that Blackness is the reason for these data points. And, again, it wouldn't be entirely incorrect. The engineering of Blackness and the depths white people will sink to keep those assigned Blackness in the lowest caste are the reasons so many of us remain ill.

So, although it might not be incorrect to say that Blackness is not Healthy, it would be incomplete. It would lack all of the ways in which society ensures that Black people never gain access to Health. It would lack complex discussions about trauma, racism, classism, weathering, the impacts of restraint, and disparities in medical provider demeanor and treatment approaches, but it wouldn't be incorrect. The United States was engineered in this way.

It would be complete to say that colonialism, white supremacy, and capitalism ensure that people assigned Blackness will never fit within the confines of Health, that we will never be healthy.

• • •

Our Healthy Kitchens, Healthy Lives panel was the penultimate plenary session of the conference. The timing was something I had questioned since the planning stages. Having a conference push the Make People Thin Again agenda for days, only to have me come in with a "Surprise! Fat people are fine when your anti-fatness and medical misogynoir don't get in the way" punchline didn't seem like good planning. I would also be discussing how pathologizing both bodies and cultural foods will result in avoidance of care for our patients a couple days after Sheila, who had declared that health disparities were too controversial, had her own session where she discussed cooking and nutrition. While preparing a, wait for it . . . kale and quinoa salad (with added edamame), she told her audience that white rice is "stripped of all nutrition" (it's not).* She

---

* In addition to energy (calories), white rice has magnesium, phosphorus, manganese, selenium, iron, folic acid, thiamin, and niacin. It's also more shelf stable than brown rice, which is an important factor for those with reduced access to food.

added that the grain is a staple of her culture and she has stopped eating it. She doubled down on the need to eliminate white rice and noodles from Asian American diets when an audience member raised their hand to share that's just not going to happen in their family and asked for ways to keep white rice and make adjustments otherwise. White rice is a staple for more than half the world's population, but Sheila didn't seem to think this was of any importance. She stressed that the ultimate goal is white rice's elimination from the diet, reinforcing the universalism often espoused in the nutrition field. And, as she had with the decision not to be on the health disparities panel, she was able to closely align with the organizers and researchers who built their brand and secured funding by problematizing people for not making the "right" choice.

I was also going to give an alternative message to the philosophy of *eat less*. In my work with clients with eating disorders, food-insecure folks, those steeped in Healthism leading to rigidity, and people whose jobs and lives don't allow for mealtimes and breaks, the majority of my time is spent figuring out ways for people to fit food into their lives rather than take it out. My work is in direct contrast to Tammy's presentation, which included her "5 Ds," which she both follows and recommends to patients when they are hungry: Distance, Delay, Distract, Dental (brush your teeth), and Drink water. Instead of giving us the 5 Ds to flag in assessing whether or not someone has an eating disorder, she was giving us the CliffsNotes for how to develop one. I'd been taking detailed notes the entire presentation, furiously writing down quotes. It was a mess. To maintain my composure that day, I left Tammy's talk and walked to a thrift store about a mile away from the conference. I found myself a red "professional" dress to work on Lexi's vision of me becoming a bawse, and grabbed a couple tops, and some baby clothes for the friend to whom I'd sent the Marco Polo videos in desperation. I bought the baby a hoodie and a pair of brown corduroy pants with the handy hammer-holding loop on it to outfit a baby butch. I felt better after the brief escape and opportunity to push my gay agenda onto the youth.

The next day, the morning of the panel, I had so much on my heart that I wanted to share and couldn't yet narrow it down. I applied the antiperspirant and put on my most capable yet casual outfit, curated by Lexi, of course. This time I wore my Chacos around the river bend and changed into my boots at the venue; genius. Luckily, the strawberry and prune smoothie had been offered at the previous day's breakfast, and today was the cashew milk yogurt drink; I could be relatively certain I wouldn't be sprinting to the restroom five minutes prior to speaking. Later that morning Eisenberg approached me just an hour prior to the panel. I was speaking to the dietitian who would join me on the panel as Eisenberg walked right toward me. I looked up to greet him but instead of speaking to me or even looking in my direction, he passed me on my right side with less than a foot of clearance, walked around me and to the other panelist, asked to speak with him privately, and ushered him away. Even by those paying me money to speak I remained invisible. It was an excellent way to tee up the panel.

And then, before I knew it, it was time. Eisenberg had the honor of introducing every other topic and speaker, expressing his deep love and appreciation, often with tears spilling from his eyes. This time was different. Walter Willett was at the podium to introduce health disparities. He shared that his keen interest in health disparities was inspired because everyone in his family is African American or Asian, a perfect get-out-of-racism-free card to play. He expressed his despair at what was happening in "their" communities during the COVID pandemic. The conference coordinator then took the mic to introduce the panelists: me, the white dietitian, and a non-Black woman of color—a food writer and culinary executive who had been a last-minute substitution on the panel after the third dietitian had a family emergency. Then the questions began. It went by both quickly and at a snail's pace. As planned, I stuck to the narratives addressing the systemic issues I see in the medical field. I shared that we aren't going to solve them by telling everyone to eat only whole grains, fruit, vegetables, nuts, seeds, legumes, and copious amounts of olive oil. Cooking skills are important, and they won't address the public health "crisis" the conference had continued to dwell upon. I remember telling the audience that I can reasonably assume that people don't get into medicine with the primary purpose to shrink their patients, and invited them to reflect on what they could be doing in their practice to provide *care*.

I spoke to the audience about the impacts of pathologizing people's bodies by diagnosing "obesity." I shared patient stories of people who delayed seeking care because of experiences of anti-fatness during medical appointments and who consequently died younger from preventable causes than those who hadn't faced such barriers. I noted that this, in and of itself, contributes to the statistics that fatness kills people versus anti-fatness killing people. I shared that the conference seemed to rely on shame as a motivator when we know that it has the opposite outcome. I talked about trauma and how we're not doing our job if we can't speak directly about its impact. Someone asked me about the Health at Every Size (HAES) framework specifically. The framework is a weight-neutral approach to health care that focuses on eating and physical activity rather than weight. I recall saying that Health at Every Size is a good place to start when looking for other ways to practice medicine and that the research on weight stigma and work like Flegal's are important to the field. I shared my belief that Health at Every Size continues the ideology of Healthism, simply including more size diversity and weight inclusivity under the umbrella of Health. I mentioned that it wasn't for me, but others find it helpful.

Lastly, I remember sharing with everyone that Africa is a continent; that all of Africa doesn't have the same "African heritage" diet referenced throughout the conference. Throughout the panel, I was looking at the audience's faces. Most expressions were confused, and rightfully so. Even if they'd been interested in the topic, the timing of this discussion likely seemed odd. I challenged much of what was pitched as the solution at the conference.

When the panel concluded, Willett returned to the podium and told the audience that the conversation was important to have. He turned toward the stage, explicitly thanked the other dietitian for his valuable contributions and insight, and concluded the session.

The end.

He left the stage.

No mention of myself or the Brown woman. It was simply over. There was no need for us to exist in Willett's world, nor on that panel. Tied to the idea that the scientific work of others and philosophies like mine are "dangerous," he ignored us in accordance with his values—and his funding.[14] We were a distraction from the messages about the Health that HKHL needed to promote. The other panelist and I were dismissed as faculty members that day, literally and figuratively; we weren't allowed to be the experts of our own experiences. Of course we weren't. And, unfortunately, it was nothing new for me.

Similar to Tammy's parading me and my philosophy around the conference, this panel positioned me to be a spectacle as well. The organizers knew about each of the presentations earlier in the conference and they knew what I was going to say and that it would come at the end. They had been correct. This was a conversation people needed to have, and asking me to show up and light everything on fire was the dramatic finale to a very lackluster conference.

Months after speaking, I had time to do a quick scan of the conference attendee feedback. It was all over the place, as is typical for things that are *too controversial*. It ranged from "Jessica Wilson's contributions were excellent. She deserves her own lecture, not just a place on a panel" to "I loved that finally a black human was part of this conference! I could not help but notice we needed more diversity in the faculty—especially when the attendees were relatively diverse. However, Jessica's angry approach balking at 'research-informed' approaches was off-putting and I felt her opinions were non-scientific but personal."

No surprises here.

Passion, when expressed by Black women, is off-putting and interpreted as anger.

Balking at decades-old data conducted primarily on middle-aged white men is literally what I said I would be doing on that panel. There should not have been surprises.

And, yes, what I shared is absolutely, unequivocally personal.

When Black women are consistently and purposefully left out of research, when we are blamed and shamed for being unwell, when we are dismissed as not feeling pain, when we *are* the research,* and when our experiences of living under white supremacy are never in consideration, it only makes sense that this is personal. How could it not be personal? What a luxury it would be to have a neutral experience in the medical-industrial complex.

Though I do not know if I will be invited back to speak at the conference, I do know that when researchers, policymakers, journalists, professors, and medical providers rely only on what research institutions have deemed worthy of funding, marginalized people will never, ever get the care we need.

---

* Henrietta Lacks and enslaved women being the test subjects for today's gynecological understandings, and many others.

chapter eight

Gooped, but Not Well

THE DAY BEGAN WITH MEDITATION.

Not just any meditation.

I was one of about two hundred people nestled under a white event tent. After grabbing a beetroot latte from the coffee cart out front, I found my friend Natalie in one of the back few rows. I squeezed in front of her, my latte and a chia seed pudding swiped from the snack table in hand, and plopped into my plastic folding chair. Ready to consume the snacks and the Wellness they would provide, I settled in; we were on a stretch of asphalt at the Porsche Experience Center in Carson, California.

The 2021 In Goop Health summit was just getting started. After thanking Porsche, the sponsor of the event, for "being so aligned with us on the theme of dreams and dreaming big and dreaming your way into new incarnations of yourself," Gwyneth Paltrow introduced Sebene Selassie to kick off the event.

I was ready.

Selassie prepared us for meditation. The group (99 percent women, likely 90 percent of whom had straight hair, cut just below the shoulder) was invited to close our eyes and shift our bodies so that both feet rested, gently, on the ground (roadway). We took a collective breath in and Selassie began in soothing slow, low tones. I was there to take it all in, through one nostril and out the other.

She started by having us connect to what drives us and asked us to draw on power and vitality. She made the connection between Porsche driving and a divine experience.

I opened one eye.

She likened this Wellness event to driving, both being a "visceral experience to unlock potential."

I opened the other eye.

We were reminded that living life is similar to driving a sports car. When driving, we need to care for those around us, we need to care for the collective; life is not about individualism.

It was my first Porsche-inspired meditation, and I knew things could only get better from there.

. . .

WHEN I SHARE MY THOUGHTS ABOUT HEALTH AND HEALTHISM with colleagues and friends, oftentimes people will listen and agree. The responses range, but many will say that they choose Wellness versus Health because it provides a more "holistic alternative." It's a different, better Way to care for a body.

My direct experience with Wellness had come from clients, social media ads, and "natural Wellness" advocates on the internet espousing the need to cut 109 ingredients from their diet to be Well. I had also had multiple conversations with people selling teas and tinctures for "detox" but who could never tell me what a detox was or how it worked better than my liver, skin, lungs, and kidneys to "detox" my body. And then there were the supplements peddled by Dr. Oz. I didn't think this was a representative sample, so I decided to learn more.

I went right to the source. Goop, Gwyneth Paltrow's "modern lifestyle brand," named after her initials, is "cutting-edge wellness advice from doctors, vetted travel recommendations, and a curated shop of clean beauty, fashion, and home."[1] I had heard of Paltrow's yoni egg, and her seventy-five-dollar This Smells Like My Orgasm candle had just hit the market at the time I decided to sign up for her 2021 In Goop Health summit. I was intrigued.

I was, honestly, a bit afraid to immerse myself in Wellness, and I didn't think I would be able to fully experience all that LA had to offer without taking twenty-seven Lyft rides each day. My friend Natalie is a pop culture enthusiast, so she was the first person I invited to join the immersion. Natalie is a white fat friend of mine I had met in the Health at Every Size community when I lived in the Bay Area; our critiques of the framework and our community organizing made us friends. I think her initial response to my Goop invitation was "That would be fascinating as a fat person." She was in.

With #VERYFAT #VERYBRAVE on the dashboard, we set out on our road trip. We stopped at a gas station in the Central Valley that also served as the local thrift shop, hosting a screaming deal on your grandmother's crystal goblets and sterling silver flatware; I loved it. We rolled into LA on a Friday to get fully immersed for the main event Sunday.

We made it through LA traffic and into the Plus Bus Boutique before anyone's bladder burst. We scored some good items, including a sequined bag—sparkles are one of my love languages. While at the register, we discovered that the blue tie-dye pants Natalie had just purchased were formerly owned by Nicole Byer. It was confirmation that Natalie was #brave for joining me for what was certainly going to be a thin woman's convention.

Saturday we traveled our way through Goop's Health Conscious Los Angeles Guide and our first stop was obviously the Detox Market to get our heads in the game. It had a myriad of products to detox our lives, including makeup foundation made from quinoa water. It was a vibe. We visited Moon Juice on our tour, a "contemporary spot serving cold-pressed juices & milks crafted from unique organic ingredients." We bought some activated snacks and adaptogenic beverages for the rest of the weekend. Natalie bought some "cookie dough," and I went all in on a chocolate mint keto smoothie for a morning snack and a "cinnamon roll" and date shake for later. I also grabbed an assortment of Moon Dusts for souvenirs. Dusts are "adaptogenic blends for your everyday bev. Moon Dust targets stress to transform your Sex, Brain, Spirit, Sleep, Power and Beauty."[2] Got it? We decided not to buy the Moon Juice Holy Yoni drops meant for "daily maintenance." We stopped into a "natural beauty" shop on the way to get lunch at Kreation Kafe & Juicery. I was completely overwhelmed at the Wellness options on the menu, including their boldly named "Berryatric" smoothie and their organic Poop Enforcer herbal tea.

Natalie had a great time laughing at me as I sputtered out my order for an o-mega bowl.

We wandered through the neighborhoods of West Hollywood and Silver Lake. We were clearly visitors in those areas; people dining and drinking coffee on sidewalk spaces would turn their heads and do a full neck swivel to watch us walk past. Nearly everyone was very thin and looked like they were ready to stop, drop, and roll into an Instagram photo shoot any moment; we were not. The Goop Guide to shops and neighborhoods didn't take us past any homeless camps and we weren't ever asked for money or food, something that was common during our time living in big cities. It felt like we were literally removed from reality.

• • •

THE MORNING OF THE GOOP SUMMIT, I GOT UP AND MADE COFFEE in which to sprinkle my Sex Dust, a "stimulating blend of adaptogens and herbs that target stress to support healthy hormonal balance, libido, and creative energy."* I was specifically going for the creative energy during the summit.

I made a premium, Keurig cup of Starbucks coffee, likely *exactly* what Amanda Chantal Bacon, founder of Moon Juice, had in mind when suggesting that her dusts be mixed into coffee or tea. I'm not sure what I was imagining dust would look like, but what spilled out of the plum-colored packet and into my mug looked exactly like the gray fluff from my vacuum cleaner. I sprinkled it in, gave

---

* These statements have not been evaluated by the Food and Drug Administration. This product is not intended to diagnose, treat, cure, or prevent any disease (https:// moonjuice.com/en-ca/products/sex-dust).

it a couple swirls with a spoon, and took a sip. It tasted a bit gritty and a bit funky. I grabbed my cinnamon roll and date shake and we headed out to the summit. On the way I spilled the coffee on my white shirt; we were off to a dusty start!

．．．

AFTER THE OPENING MEDITATION, WE WERE DIVIDED INTO GROUPS by wristband color. Natalie and I were in the green group and were shepherded to our workshop with astrologer Chani Nicholas by a fellow who signaled his green leader status to us with a green hankie in his back pocket.

After learning more about our sun and moon signs, we followed the green hankie to the front of the building for the driving porscheon (sorry, not sorry) of the summit. Sans driver's license, something prohibited because of my seizures, I was unable to access the "mind-body thrill of driving a sports car" so advertised as part of this program and was left to my own devices. The blue team was taking its turn through the expo space, and they were keeping a tight handle on which colors went where (the irony). As I could not mix and mingle, I took the opportunity to ask the green team shepherd about his job. He gushed about Goop. He volunteered to staff the event because he loves the culture and the company's willingness to "ask the hard questions." It was almost line for line what Goop claims to be about, coming from a place of "curiosity and nonjudgment, and we start hard conversations, crack open taboos, and look for connection and resonance everywhere we can find it. We don't mind being the tip of the spear—in short, we go first so you don't have to. We're glad you're here."

Hmmm.

Anyhow, I *was* glad I was there; there were free snacks. It was noon and I was hungry. Per our schedule, our lunch was at two p.m., and, if you know me, two p.m. is not a lunchtime I can get behind, so I followed the green hankie man to the snack area. My choices included a crudité box, mini baked goods, a nut mix, and a sparkling collagen tea. I grabbed the last three, all the while grateful for the "cinnamon roll" and date shake I had stashed in my bag. I inhaled a muffin, specifically the "healthy banana muffin, *gf, *df, *nf, *v," and decided to try the date shake made with almond milk, cold brew coffee, dates, almond butter, and Sex Dust.

I took a seat in the lobby and took a swig. It was one of the most okayish things I'd consumed the whole trip. It could have been good, even, without the dusty, gritty aftertaste.

It was an experience, perhaps not the Porsche Driving Experience I was watching unfold through the lobby window, but a different mind-body experience nonetheless.

· · ·

Natalie returned with the green team after their driving adventures and I was released from the holding area. It was our turn on the expo floor.

Collagen mocktails, facial massages, embroidered pillow mountains to climb on, silk sleep masks, so many things to choose from, but the Hydration Room's pop-up shop was the highlight for me. It was one of the smaller stations; the only real notable thing about it was the syringes filled with dark red liquid and people in scrubs standing by.

Blood? Beetroot tonics?

Incorrect.

These were B_{12} injections and they were offered to any of us who wanted to pull down our pants or roll up our sleeves in an open-air expo.

The injections were supposed to be as harmless as a multivitamin, with a promised boost of unparalleled energy. I was here for the full immersion, so I turned my back to all of the participants and unbuttoned my jeggings to expose the top of my hip. The tech rubbed alcohol on me, pinched the injection site a couple times, and stuck me with the needle. It took a few seconds to empty the syringe, and it wasn't any more painful than a typical shot.

We were told to expect a boost in our energy soon, likely within the next twenty-four hours. I asked how often people got injections and was told that customers visit any of the LA-area Hydration Rooms for B_{12} injections every two to three days or one time a week, depending on how quickly their energy drains. I was fascinated that people made time for injections multiple times a week.

I checked out the pamphlet and realized how out of the Wellness loop I was. The company offered a variety of IV therapies for basic cold/flu, hangovers, jet lag, fitness recovery, and much more. My favorite offering was the most specific: the Celebration IV that will "improve your energy, reduce stress and provide immune support for an upcoming event or trade show all for $250."[3] The trade show specificity captured my imagination and made me think of people getting ready for LA Fashion Week, the Oscars, or something similar. The company also offered mobile services that would come to your workplace; all of this reinforced my LA anxiety and fascination.

. . .

Post-injection, our lunchtime had finally arrived. We were served food from Goop Kitchen that I would loosely call a meal, but perhaps "glorified snack" is a better description. There were items I could not identify but consumed nonetheless. There was definitely salmon in the container and the brown rice was recognizable. There were brown chunky things cut into three-inch strips, and 30 percent of people on Instagram thought it was a mushroom; I think the rest were as confused as I was. We got some coconut date cookies and were saved by a berry smoothie—nothing fancy, dust-free, and delicious.

We were scheduled for two more workshops before we returned to the big tent for Paltrow's closing events and remarks. Dr. Srini Pillay, psychiatrist and brain researcher "with 'renaissance man' bona fides," spoke to us about cultivating creativity and finding our hidden potential. There were overtones of needing to take personal responsibility to find said hidden potential, including the advice to stop "living from a victimized identity" in order to get creative. He told us that we all have the time to get creative, we just need to prioritize it. And he advised us to step into our greatness and recognize when we "[hold ourselves] back from walking into possibility." We were to be inspired by the life and work of Elon Musk whose "greatness is an incredible social service." Absolutely not.

There were moments during the day when I remembered who I am and where I was, and this was one of them. Astrology, free snacks, and wearing sleep masks could be applied to our lives broadly. However, there were likely people on my green team who were inspired by Musk, a billionaire who tells the world he is "cash-poor" but sells his houses, throws tantrums about COVID stay-at-home orders, remains staunchly against union organizing, and thinks he can buy free speech.[4]

There were likely those on the green team who could simply choose creativity after hearing Pillay tell us that we need to stop worrying, generally, because it is a "crutch." These same folks might be able to add three "compulsory" twenty-minute creative breaks each day, more than most people's days allow for a meal. I recall myself looking around the room and wondering who this talk was for.

The last workshop the green team attended together was "Getting the Love You Want" with Dr. Nasserzadeh, who talked about different types of love, finding a good fit in love through which we are thriving, and regularly reassessing relationships. She asked us what we are proud of, about our essences, congruency, conflict, appreciation, and reward. She left us with the challenge to assess where we are in our romantic relationships and to write both the love story we deserve and the love story we desire. If we were the one to create the narrative going forward, what would it be?

The day ended with Paltrow having intimate conversations with UC Berkeley neuroscience and psychology professor Matthew Walker, PhD, whose book *Why We Sleep*, which has been subject to controversy, was in our Goop swag bag. Paltrow was also joined on stage by Jay Shetty, a friend and fan of hers and also a former monk. Paltrow glamorized his choice to "get rid of material possessions" when entering a monastery; the irony of more than one thousand dollars' worth of material possessions in our swag bag was not lost on me. Shetty praised Paltrow for "introducing people" to topics that are taboo and not discussed; we all need to expose and explore things that are different and unique and, turning to Paltrow, said, "That's what your work is doing."

That statement got me thinking about Wellness as a construction, and how one thin, rich, basic white woman can write the story of what being Well looks like in the West; Well exists in the ways influencers say it exists. It makes sense, though. How we view bodies has always been constructed; history repeats itself unless interrupted. White women reinforce and enforce the expectations for whiteness among themselves. Wellness—the use of hundreds of dollars of products every day just to put on your face, the use of dusts and powders to make "meals," the fact that these retailers only have stores in cities and areas that cater to rich white people—is peak whiteness. To achieve it demands that we be invested in the idea that our bodies need taming, this time with a variety of "practices" instead of simply counts, measures, or principles.

Wellness requires persistence to achieve its promises. As much as Gwyneth has Goop to perform peak whiteness, Kourtney Kardashian now has Poosh, "the modern guide to living your best life" where you can "Poosh Your Wellness." She created it because she felt that "healthy living" gets a bad rap when it can be cool and sexy; her curations will help us bridge the gap.[5] The two have even collaborated on the "This Smells Like My Pooshy" candle. There are now multiple white women who are brands in and of themselves, attempting to offer others hope that they might attain the desirability and social status of Gwyneth and Kourtney.

Wellness ups the ante on Health. Wellness is the peak way to have a body, a body that conforms to all norms, those of the past and those created. Wellness, when defined by influencers, which most of the time it is, is incredibly expensive. For those in the middle and lower classes who are able to achieve or perform Health, white women's Wellness is the highest standard for having a good, obedient body. Bodies must not age, sag, or wrinkle, and don't worry—we can buy an eighty-five-dollar face spatula to prevent part of this. Wellness is not simply beauty, it is a cocktail of products and rituals that we need to spend hundreds of dollars on and perform daily to show our devotion to desirability politics and attempts to attain the social capital and relevance reserved for celebrities.

Anyone who has seen Beyoncé's *Homecoming* documentary knows what Black women will put our bodies through in order to conform to what is demanded—to maintain social and financial capital. Her restriction and "practices" almost killed her, yet she endured. Though, at the same time, having put her body through all of that, having done everything demanded of her by whiteness, she will never be granted access to the highest caste. She will have participated in the respectability required of Black women to get a seat at the Wellness table. Wellness raises the bar for whiteness, and offers products to achieve it, but will never grant access to Black women in the end.

There are efforts to make Wellness more accessible, to deconstruct it, to rethink it. And I ask why. Finding a way to squeeze into yet another table that wasn't built for our vibrancy sounds like effort that could be better spent radically reimagining a world in which we don't need Wellness.

By the end of the Goop summit, we had done it all. The Disneyland of Wellness was closing. Natalie and I grabbed our giant swag bags and headed back to the Airbnb. I was ready to go to bed and wake up feeling refreshed and extra energized from the injection and whatever it is that collagen is supposed to help with. It was both everything and nothing that I expected. I had lived, laughed, and loved that day and got a glimpse of what it would mean to live a life of ease. I was able to exist as a very basic bitch that day.

But one question lingered.

Who is Wellness for?

. . .

I WOKE UP MONDAY WITH PART OF MY QUESTION ANSWERED.

I didn't have a dewy glow. I felt like garbage, after said garbage had been driven over by a . . . Porsche SUV.

Sitting up in bed, I immediately started having auras left and right. This hadn't happened to me in my twenty-eight years of having seizures. My brain was foggy and easily distracted by hyperfocusing moment to moment to brace for a seizure. My eye was twitching, which is my primary indicator of work stress. This didn't make sense after having done nothing but heartily enjoy the past three days, and not being at all hypervigilant. It was confusing. A seizure flare wasn't the promise I had been sold the previous day. I was supposed to feel energized and alert. Quite the opposite had happened. So much for my Live, Laugh, Love attempt to be Well.

I took a half dose of my rescue meds that morning. This can typically keep my seizures at bay until I can rest and/or destress; they also can make things a bit fuzzy, though still functional. The amount to take was a deliberation. I had a whole day of Wellness still ahead and I wanted to stay as present as possible.

I am very grateful for that tiny white pill. A product of Western medicine, it provides some assurance that I won't walk out into

traffic, fall off my bike, or wake up on a park bench with my belongings stolen if I have a seizure. My prescriptions are not part of a
"practice" or a "journey." They're a part of my morning and evening
routines. Perhaps you've seen photos or caricatures with medication
on one side and vegetables on the other presenting a dichotomous
choice between pills or peppers. I've got three words for you: Give Me
Pills. Vegetables will do nothing to regulate my temporal lobe.

After taking the medication, my auras didn't quite go away, but I
was willing to see whether more Wellness could help me out. After
all, I was resilient.

I had scheduled a SoulCycle class that morning at the suggestion
of multiple people when they heard of this project. It was good
timing in the itinerary; the endorphins from exercise typically hold
off a seizure for the rest of the day. Natalie dropped me off at the
outdoor SoulCycle studio on her way back to reality, and I was on
my own for the rest of the trip.

The class was everything I had hoped for. Multiple times the instructor warned the class of eight people, "Don't waste your time
by coming here and not putting in the work!" And that coming
there and not "trying" was just a waste of time. All while a quick
scan around the space indicated that I was the only one not jostling
in sync to the choreography cues that others had clearly practiced.
The experience was absolutely not a waste of time; it fit right in to
the culty vibes I was getting from this immersion. Following the
class I decided to refresh myself with the sparkling collagen tea I
had taken from the summit. The tall, slim yellow can spoke to me,
literally: "Hello, liquid radiance" was spelled out under the list of
ingredients. It was . . . collageny? It was bubbly and tangy with an
odd aftertaste. Hello, Wellness.

I left the outdoor studio, changed clothes, and started my stroll to lunch and promptly my auras returned. At first I tried to press on; surely they must go away soon? My spouse called and I was grateful that she was "with" me; if something happened, someone would notice. I kept walking, against my best judgment, but by the time I approached a park, it was time to sit my ass down and call the friend I was meeting and ask her for a ride. It was my first time meeting Anna in person, having built a friendship talking about bodies and how eating disorder treatment frameworks even fail those for whom they are designed. I really didn't want our first intro to start with me asking for her help. My internalized ableism adds a huge scoop of shame when asking for assistance and piles on my need to be resilient.

It got to the point where I was feeling unsafe with my lacking processing abilities, so I phoned Anna. And, of course, it was no big deal for her to pick me up. We caught up at Café Gratitude, a restaurant that aims "to create a healthier, more vibrant world by inviting more people into the simple pleasures of clean, plant-based nutrition." Over an "I am Humble" plate with added coconut "bacon," and an "I am Cosmic" spirulina latte—all of the ingredients for a well-rounded Wellness meal—we lived, laughed, loved our way through "lunch." I was committed to seeing how the Well lived and Anna gave me the hippie history of Venice Beach and how the Wellness vibe came to be. This was an experiment that I could not quit, especially because I was feeling . . . unwell. I could push through, I always did, didn't I? After lunch Anna dropped me off at my hotel, and we shared a hug, which is the last thing I clearly remember that day.

I had made it to a safe place. As typically happens, my brain had been surviving all day, and, at the first opportunity for me to relax I had a seizure. My first that evening. I don't remember when I had the second one. My short-term memory after a seizure is minimal at best, and having another meant that the entire evening was hazy. All I remember is needing to find something for dinner in line with the Wellness immersion. I didn't have the cognitive processing to think through an alternative plan like getting something at the hotel. My seizure brain struggles enough to remember the previous plan and can't integrate any new information. I remember wandering around Venice Beach, following the direction the blue dot on Google Maps was trying to take me. I took a TikTok video of me trying my beet and kelp burger to which I added adzuki "bacon," and that's the entire "memory" I have except for the migraine that evening.

My recollection of Monday and Tuesday relies on the many photos taken, texts, phone calls, and conversations. The in-between spaces are unaccounted for. I hope I took a nap or two, but I really don't know. My cell phone location was turned on and I was checking in with my family when I'd leave the hotel and return. My left arm was numb-to-tingly all of Tuesday, a symptom that began in July 2021 during the flare that took me out of work for that August. Yay, bodies.

It wasn't until Wednesday that I woke up feeling like my typical self. Was it because I destroyed a full plate of not-vegan chicken nachos for dinner Tuesday? Perhaps.

● ● ●

PEOPLE FOLLOWING THIS TRIP ON SOCIAL MEDIA KEPT ASKING, "But how did you *feel*?" Despite the shenanigans, did I feel amazing? Was I going to live longer?

Honestly, a not-so-small part of me hoped I would.

Maybe Wellness could cure me of my seizures. Or, if not cured, maybe I could get a longer-than-one-month break—the typical interval—between seizures. Maybe the B_{12} would eliminate the haziness and migraines after seizures. Maybe the dusts and adaptogens could reduce my prescription medication doses. A part of me wanted to join the cadres of people who claimed to manage their illnesses "holistically" and "naturally." I could become a person with a nutrition practice that I would have formerly critiqued. I could slip slowly from social media or dramatically pivot my work and start partnering with folks like J. J. Smith, the creator of Lizzo's smoothie detox.

My internalized ableism often runs wild within me. Every time a client sits down in my office and tells me they want to manage a chronic illness "naturally, without taking drugs, you know?" I'm reminded that I'm what people are trying not to become, an unnatural pill-popper. I'm not immune to the messages of Wellness and individuals who believe I've succumbed to sick care and am "pushed through the healthcare system and loaded up with a bunch of prescriptions." I'm choosing to pollute my body and choosing to be one of those people who "deal with . . . many, potentially, nasty side effects."[6]

Oddly enough, these were not the direct messages at In Goop Health. No one brought up medications or the need to heal holistically without Western medicine. There was no overt message of Healthism at Goop. At no point did I find my internal narrative justifying my prescription drug use as I had done throughout Healthy Kitchens, Healthy Lives.

. . .

THE HEALTHY KITCHENS, HEALTHY LIVES WEBSITE CITES AN Institute of Medicine report that states "the great advances of genetics and biomedical discoveries could be more than offset by the burden of illness, disability, and death."[7] HKHL makes clear that chronically ill people, disabled people, and, well, dead people are an incredible societal burden. They're—*we're*—not able to contribute to the economy as those who have Health. We're not able to fully contribute to capitalism; we suck resources from the richest nation; we're unacceptable citizens. Our bodies are Wrong. We are blamed and assigned moral failing by those who are supposed to "care" for all bodies but refuse to do so.

The last day of the HKHL and prior to my plenary there was the one and only food insecurity plenary. I thought it would be a great intro to the panel. Brian Frank, MD, an assistant professor in the Department of Family Medicine at Oregon Health and Science University, made the case for the attendees to care about food insecurity. We were presented with a case study of a four-year-old white boy who was food insecure. I'll call him Joe. Frank led us through Joe's likely trajectory if he didn't get food assistance. Joe was labeled with behavioral problems in middle school and he didn't graduate high school because he was sick all the time. Joe became "an unstable member of the workforce" because of a variety of diseases. Joe had a heart attack in his forties and died in his sixties. Frank created an image of Joe being washed away in a sea of pills, apparently riding the wave of illness. We were told that Joe became a "drain on our healthcare system" due to his illnesses and reliance on medications. Frank told us that *this* was why we should care about food insecurity. Those of us who could afford to spend time and money in Napa would, apparently, be moved to caring about food insecurity because food-insecure people may not deliver our Amazon packages on time, and our tax dollars will subsidize their health care. That's why.

I take a total of eight prescription pills each day. I am that drain on the healthcare system; I ride the river of pills. That's me. I've had to take time off for my seizures, as previously mentioned. I am that unstable member of the workforce. So, yeah, I have internalized ableism, especially from those who are supposed to provide care. In medicine and nutrition we're told that the best way to manage conditions is through "lifestyle changes." Prescriptions are for those who have failed to try. Taking medication can carry shame and stigma for not being able to "fix" one's body on one's own.

As I will clearly never have Health, it makes sense that I, and many other Black women, would put hope into Wellness. But was this immersion what "naturally, without taking drugs," looks like? I had not tried the discount, "accessible" type of Wellness; it was five days of peak Wellness. The Real Thing. The original recipe.

And I was sicker than when I started, and, hypothetically, even more of a drain on tax dollars. "Maybe you should lay off the Wellness," said no one ever until that Tuesday when Lexi told me to stop taking the dusts and adaptogens. Shana was similarly supportive: "That makes me want to set their B_{12} on fire." I have the best friends.

Going into this I knew I wasn't healthy. It wasn't a secret. After this trip it was clear that I wasn't able to be Well either; I wasn't able to be "clean," "natural," "pure," or "holistic." And by that point, I didn't care. I was exhausted and just wanted to go home.

• • •

I LEARNED SOME THINGS ABOUT MYSELF AT GOOP, BUT THE highlights for the trip came in the moments I ventured off script.

After the mini muffin that seemed to be made of stardust, and while waiting for the return of the green team, I took in my surroundings. I was one of maybe three Black women who had paid to be Gooped, of course. The support staff for the event were predominantly Black and Brown. It was quite a juxtaposition. I was grateful I hadn't chosen to wear a black-on-black outfit that day, as I likely would have been asked to point someone in the direction of the restroom or the free snacks. Natalie was the fattest person there; our bodies were hypervisible at the event, yet also invisible. At the lunch break, Natalie and I were seated at a four-person table and were continually passed by participants who would join other tables. It wasn't until two non-Black women of color asked to join us that I got to have a meaningful conversation with someone other than the man with the green hankie. One of the women had observed that she was "the only curvy Latina" at the event. All four of us looked very different from each other and also very different from the majority of participants there.

Earlier, while I was finishing my dusty date shake in the lobby and waiting for the green group to return, I noticed a younger Black woman working adjacent to the Experience. I decided to ask her what she thought about the scenes unfolding around her. I approached her cautiously, especially aware of physical boundaries in a pandemic. She seemed open to talking to me, so I stood a few feet away and we had a conversation through our masks. She told me it had been interesting to watch the setup over the last couple days and that the people had been very nice. I asked her whether she was familiar with Paltrow or In Goop Health prior to this event. She told me that she was not, but "it must be for a good cause because it has health in the name."

I took a deep sigh and nodded.

In the midst of the Wellness circus, I had been distracted by bright and shiny objects, and her comment brought me back to why I was there. Black women are up against a narrative that tells us that our literal bodies, our selves, are risk factors for disease. Health is something we're told we need to be constantly worried about, while at the same time we're never granted access. I can see that finding Wellness offers an opportunity that going to the doctor or the clinic does not. In a society that has used Black women to advance medicine and has historically denied Black women the care more easily accessible to their white counterparts, Black women are uniquely vulnerable to something that promises the same "health benefits" but does not require the gatekeeping that medicine does. When we avoid doctor appointments because of the ways we've experienced violence from the medical establishment, we can buy Wellness products online that promise us the outcomes we would have expected to find coming from a primary care provider.

The young Black woman at Goop and I chatted for a bit longer. I asked what she thought about the demographics of the people in attendance. She was surprised because there were "so many Caucasians" there. She had never been among this many white people before, and she thought that if the event was truly about health there should be more diversity among attendees.

Correct.

I knew I would find surprises that day, but I didn't expect this conversation.

In all of the conversations I'd been having with Black women outside of my circle and with friends and colleagues, there wasn't a case for this chapter until I made it. Only in extended conversations about my ideas did they recognize that they had internalized the promises of Wellness for themselves without realizing it, and that spending fifty dollars for three items at Whole Foods would not lead them to the same purity and morality afforded to white women in society.

• • •

THE DUSTY DATE SMOOTHIES WERE AN ESSENTIAL PART OF MY immersion. Paltrow posts her breakfast smoothie recipes on Instagram and I needed to see what they were about. Yet Lizzo talked openly about drinking smoothies on Instagram and the internet panicked. What the public doesn't question for thin white women can be unacceptable for fat Black women. White women will remain the standard to which all women are subjected and Black women will never, ever be granted access to womanhood if our cultural narrative doesn't change. It's by design.

Yet. After all of this, if a dystopian future presented itself, I'd work for Goop before I worked for the Harvard School of Public Health, an institution so actively invested in the narratives that if one is ill or fat it's the individual's responsibility to fix and that shame, blame, and cooking classes are the ticket to Health.

No one at Goop mentioned "obesity," calories, weight loss, or a goal of Health. There was only one mention of weight at all, specifically by the sleep researcher saying that "healthy weight" is associated with getting enough sleep, that's it. Goop was a rich white woman's theme park, but at no point did it point the finger at those who weren't spending their money on vitamin injectables and collagen-laden products. There was no discussion about "healthy food" or "processed food." Goop never pretended to be for the "public," though it cost less to attend than HKHL did, which demonstrates HKHL's investment in educating the actual public.* If Harvard's School of Public Health was truly for the public, David Eisenberg would have heard about food apartheid prior to the conference. It's that simple.

If I worked for Goop, I would not have to work alongside a professor who doesn't seem to understand the difference between correlation and causation, the intentions of redlining, the impacts of poverty, and who told the HKHL crowd that "the state of health in America" is "in a death spiral,"[8] among many other things. In a 2015 interview with Alvin Powell for the *Harvard Gazette*, Walter Willett discussed the Supplemental Nutrition Assistance Program (SNAP)—an initiative that provides food for 9.5 million families. He said that the program "is actually fueling the obesity epidemic and we are, at the same time, paying for the consequences for that." He also said, "The food industry does not want [SNAP benefits] touched at all because it's basically a massive funnel of tens of billions of dollars into the processed food industry."[9] It seems like an understanding of, ahem, food apartheid would inspire a more nuanced discussion of why SNAP benefits might go to food items that are shelf stable, easy to prepare, and available at overpriced corner stores more often than in the produce section of a grocery store.

---

* HKHL also didn't provide a swag bag; not even a tote bag!

If I were a salesperson for Goop, I could sell a Smells Like My Orgasm candle. Working for Harvard, I'd have to peddle paternalistic and patronizing messaging.

I left HKHL with a road map for developing an eating disorder.

I left In Goop Health with a free vibrator, Paltrow's own brand.

I was close to rage-crying multiple times in Napa.

I laughed my way through Goop.

Wellness is peak whiteness and is inherently healthist, but, to my knowledge, it doesn't attempt to influence national health policies. Wellness sets an unattainable bar for people and how they should tend to their bodies. Health influences economic decisions for corporations, cities, states, and the country that people cannot escape.

I'll sell snake oil before I sell my soul.

PART 3

A NEW STORY

chapter nine

Rewriting the Narrative

The master's tools will never dismantle the master's house.

—Audre Lorde

"I JUST THINK EVERYTHING IS BETTER WHEN WE'RE NOT PER-
forming for whiteness, and every time some layer of that oppressive gaze is stripped away, like, something realer and more
interesting happens." I'd asked Shana, Fresh, and Ifasina what they
would like to see from society and humanity going forward, and
Shana blew us away with this answer.

Rewriting a collective narrative offers an opportunity for agency,
autonomy, and healing. We can absolutely rewrite our individual
narrative, but for many of us, our own story can only go so far.
How can we create communities in which the oppressive gaze is
stripped away and we might find a bit more ease?

• • •

"One thing I know about Black folks is that we give a fuck about each other," Ifasina shared with us.

Rewriting what it means to care about each other while under white supremacy could mean we acknowledge the safety found in strategies like respectability, while still allowing space for agency. We can share the expectations that whiteness has for Blackness in a way that lets people make informed choices about whether or not to participate in that performance. We can stop policing dichotomies deciding who is a Queen and who is in Queen Training. When we offer a choice rather than A Way, we don't need to surveil those of us who laugh loudly, ask questions, have dyed their hair blond, show their asses in oversized T-shirts, and wear bonnets or slippers in the airport. There is opportunity to discuss the royalty that Black women in fact are, without tying that designation to whether or not we conform to what whiteness demands. When we know that regardless of whether we're in a bonnet or business suit our bodies will continue to be deemed unruly and that we will never make it to the top of the caste pyramid, there is a freedom that comes. No longer is there only one path to existence and success. No longer do we need to feel shame for just being.

Ifasina offered the following to our elders who have been bound by the rules of respectability and impose the same restrictions onto others: "I want to belong to you different, sis. That's how I feel. I get it. . . . You feel like I belong to you. We belong to each other. You going about this in a way I don't consent to. I want to belong to you different. Let's belong to each other in collective liberation." We can truly be together in collective liberation.

• • •

REWRITING HOW WE TALK ABOUT BODIES OFFERS AN EXAMINATION into why we separate our "true selves" from our body.

In 2016, I attended a performance by Sins Invalid, "a disability justice based performance project that incubates and celebrates artists with disabilities, centralizing artists of color and LGBTQ/gender-variant artists as communities who have been historically marginalized."[1] The show was a beautiful, magical collection of different artists with varying degrees of ability; there were many moments that moved me to tears. During one performance, I remember the crowd gasping as the assumed-to-be-non-disabled ballet dancers went to sing the song they were dancing to aloud and the music cut, and the crowd realized the artists were deaf.

A couple days later I was back in the Bay Area volunteering for the same event, providing access support backstage. I helped people in and out of costumes, let people know when their performance was coming up, and got to know some of the performers and activists. I hadn't realized how much the show had impacted me until I got back to my friend's place that night. Luckily, he wasn't home. I stood before his full-length mirror and a very, verrrry ugly cry escaped me. I was furious; how dare they be unapologetic about their disabilities!? How could they possibly celebrate something that I was constantly trying to separate myself from?! I was staring in the mirror looking at the body I so often didn't want to be mine. Didn't they know that I was literally killing myself *and* lying to myself believing that what I was doing was working!? My internalized ableism overfloweth. I'd made many poor decisions following seizures that put me in danger just so I could keep going, believing that everything was fiiiiiine. I sat down on my friend's cold floor and put my head in my hands and prepared for the emotional awakening to take a while and take its toll. The next morning was the first time I, with incredibly puffy and red eyes, referred to myself as a sick/chronically ill person, an identity that I continue to orient myself toward and embrace.

Sitting on the cold floor, among the dirt and dog hair, I'd realized that when I view myself as *existing* in a body that has seizures or *occupying* a body that is chronically ill, I become who I am *in spite of* my seizures rather than *because* of them. If I exist in an ill body, I talk about my body like it's a weird fleshy suit that I zip up in the morning; I distance myself from the reality that my body is me; I reinforce my internalized ableism. But I am who I am because my seizures have touched every decision I've made in my life at one point or another. My seizures impact both if and how I navigate the world every day and all of the challenges and opportunities that have come as a result.

I cannot say that embodying epilepsy or my Sick identity has made it any easier to *be* Sick. But I do have a bit more compassion for myself during my meltdowns, rather than blaming my body for not living up to what I expect it to do. Embodiment hasn't made it easier to ask for help; well, maybe a little, but I am far more likely to rant about my internalized ableism *while* asking for help. I will grit my teeth while asking for a ride or for someone to run an errand for me because it's one hundred degrees out and walking or biking is surely a bad idea. I'm still awkward about it. I sometimes text my spouse while we're in the same small house to ask for help so it appears like a casual request rather than something I agonized over for thirty-seven straight minutes before asking.

Per their website, Sins Invalid "recognizes that we will be liberated as whole beings—as disabled, as queer, as brown, as black, as gender non-conforming, as trans, as women, as men, as non-binary gendered—we are far greater whole than partitioned." It's like they could foresee my impending meltdown.

There are many reasons that someone may not want to demographically identify with their body; agency and autonomy in the choice to identify are essential. Some people may find emotional safety in the separation between the self and the body for a variety of reasons. I found some emotional safety in lying to myself and others for decades and stretching myself much further than was needed rather than admit I needed help, that I was vulnerable. Escaping one's body can be an effective strategy for those who have experienced trauma. Separating the body from the self can also be spiritually relevant in some religions. People's autonomy with how they identify is essential, it's an important part of their body story that they get to tell. Hopefully, we can be intentional with our language when we talk about people and remember how rarely we hear of people who *occupy* a cis-het body or a thin, non-disabled body. Not until recently did news outlets start naming suspects and/or police officers' whiteness as an identity. Reporters would say "female suspect" for a white person or "Black female suspect"; the same for police officers. Those folks are the default to whom all others are compared.

Where can we find the opportunity in rewriting what it means to *be*?

The language and tools we have developed subtly place blame on our bodies rather than on the systems and structures that originally wrote the narratives. Caste lives on the body, but it is not *because* of the body. It is because society has assigned meaning to the body. It is the fluid assignment of race, fatness, gender, disability, sexuality, among many other social constructions, that impacts Health and humanity, or lack thereof, not those demographics in and of themselves.

. . .

Rewriting how we talk about food leaves space for us to enjoy it without overthinking it. My friend Alison, someone I met in 2020 due to our passion for conversations about bodies and creating safer environments for people, once told me that my message is, "'Eat food and feel how it feels' . . . and that's terrifying!" And I get it. Going from guardrails into an abyss of eating all of the foods can be scary. And I've seen a burden lifted when people Eat Food and have it not be assigned meaning created by internal narratives and artificial rules. When people eat without needing a road map, when people eat and see how it goes, and adjust accordingly. When people notice when societal messages get in the way of finishing something as amazing as a burrito. Feeding a body is hard; can we find a bit more ease?

I continue to rewrite what it means to be a clinician.

I think of myself as a regular-degular clinician. My clients would confirm that I wear Chacos (with the double strap because they're fancier . . . ?) for 95 percent of my in-person appointments. I have visible tattoos; I don't typically wear makeup. I'm in my forties and still don't know what "business casual" means; is it khakis? Dockers? I *am* clear about casual, though; that's what I give. I deeply believe that how clinicians show up in a room matters.

I was once talking with a fat client about being the "only one" in mixed spaces. They had been the only fat client at a residential eating disorder treatment and *no one* brought it up. None of their thin therapists addressed how it impacts the therapeutic relationship and how being fat among a group of thin people trying desperately not to be fat shows up in group therapy and is inherently harmful. On top of that, their current outpatient therapist hadn't brought it up either. There seemed to be good rapport between the client and their therapist, and I asked the client whether they could bring it up.

"Have you met her!?" they asked me.

"No," I replied. "I've only spoken to her on the phone."

"Well, she's *very* thin and *very* well put together."

I understood that, no, they weren't going to bring it up. By all accounts, I'm not *very* well put together, and in that moment I realized how important it was. The client shared that they didn't think I was pretending to be someone that I'm not while in the office. I'm not tightly contained and the art on the walls, the stacks of paper behind me, and the ten different sweaters on the hook on the back of my door demonstrate as much. They told me that they believe I'm the same person in my work that I am in my day-to-day interactions, and this provided a sense of ease. I wasn't performing, so they didn't have to perform in my office either. They could get the care they deserved while not being afraid to bring their whole self, something they're still working on being able to do.

I'm not a *meet them where they are in their process* flavor of dietitian, as most of my colleagues describe themselves. I find that meeting clients in their beliefs about their eating can place ownership on them and increase self-blame. Meeting them where they are often looks like matching their level of distress about their eating patterns and inadvertently problematizing them when, instead, there is variation in all that humans experience and in our eating patterns. A frequent example I hear is the distress at finishing the entire pint of (actual, not diet) ice cream. I've found that, for some people, seeing the bottom of the carton means so much more than needing to put the carton in the trash rather than in the freezer, often setting clients up for a shame spiral with a cascade of compensatory thoughts and actions. It would be easy for me to match their distress, to use a therapeutic tool or a principle to prevent them from ever seeing the bottom of that carton again after starting at the top. But instead I try to norm that experience and to reduce shame, to provide context. I've used the example of having been a student at UC Davis and shared that at times my housemates and I would look forward to the Pint for a Pint blood donation drives on campus for two primary reasons: the free snacks while they make you sit for fifteen minutes afterward and the coupon for a Baskin Robbins pint of ice cream for our pint of blood. We'd meet up at the ice cream shop those evenings, make our ice cream choices, and sit on the curb outside and finish our pints. And then we'd go home. The end. It was a bright spot in an otherwise grueling academic quarter. I ask my clients whether my housemates and I should have been distressed about this; they always reply that we shouldn't have been concerned. My clients and I then discuss how context impacts how we view our actions and reactions. We work to discover what stories we've decided to adopt and what would need to shift in order to let them go.

When clients and colleagues describe my work, they say that I'm direct; I've even used it to describe myself. But in writing this book and paying more attention to what I say with clients, I think that it's more accurate to say that I'm clear. I like to think that I use words that mean things. That I'm not ambiguous, and I don't require clients to interpret the meaning of my words.

A highly skilled colleague of mine, who doesn't use intuitive eating with her clients, suggests that they engage with the concept that "Every body part gets a vote" when deciding what to eat.

I ran this by one friend who is doing relatively well in her eating disorder recovery. She was confused. "So, like, my thigh is hungry, but my calf is not?"

I presented it to another friend with a long history of chronic dieting and weight cycling, who was similarly confused. "Like, *every* body part?"

"That's what she said," I replied. "Your head wants one thing and your belly may want another."

My friend told me that's too much to think about. Her goal is to *not* overthink and analyze her food choices because that was, and continues to be, her default from years of intentional weight loss attempts. Her goal is to eat food that tastes good, which sounds like an excellent strategy to me.

I like to think that I string words together in a way that is helpful for my clients. My most common line for *all* of my clients is "Please eat more food."

The majority of my job is working with people who might benefit from eating more food—be it all day long, for meals, for snacks, and/or earlier in the day. Hanger prevention and addressing energy deficits are core components of my work. For some clients, this isn't a big ask and they're able to connect how eating more can help get them through the day with the capacity they need. They know what "more" looks like, have access to food, and just need support figuring out where to fit it into their day and how to plan ahead. Some need support with getting safe housing. We discuss which foods are more calorically dense when clients have limited resources. Some clients, especially those who have recently been eating with a goal of shrinking themselves, are more confused about what meals and snacks might look like.

Some dietitians, even those who consider themselves on the cutting edge, still use more directive approaches. The plate model of portioning is still in use, and some dietitians prescribe meal plans for people.

I, as you can imagine, do not. I don't see the value in telling people exactly how much they should eat, especially in the context of biological variability and shaky research on standardized caloric intake. Prescriptive methods lead to the inevitable outcome of there being a "too much" amount of food to eat, even with intuitive eating, which is like every method we've been told to use to restrain and restrict ourselves. This also positions me in the place of knowing exactly what someone else's body needs, which is ridiculous, as evidenced by every contradictory nutrition research paper available.

Both clients and colleagues ask how I do this. I think it's simple. I have also found that it is clear.

Josh and I were reflective about food containers; we talked about how much he would pack for someone else's lunch. When a client with a history of restriction tells me what they had for lunch and asks for my thoughts, I start by being curious: "Is that what you would pack for a friend's lunch?" or "Might you pack that amount of food for a child's snack?" When someone tells me what they ate for dinner, I may follow up with, "If you were having a date over for dinner, what would you serve them?" We discuss the multiple components they would put on a plate if they were to cook for someone else. I ask questions that I hope inspire reflection, which leaves room for self-assessment. I try to remove myself from being the one who knows. If they're unsure about the answers, I remain curious. "What do you think would happen if you only fed a friend six vegan chicken nuggets or carrots and hummus for dinner?" They are usually aware that others would likely stop at In-N-Out Burger on the way home because they'd still be hungry.

I find that asking these questions does not elicit defensiveness. It doesn't create resistance. It doesn't leave room for a standoff between dietitian and client.

A colleague of mine asked me how I would approach a client who reported bingeing on a whole large bag of chips and presented in distress. She had asked a recent client, "How did it feel to binge last night?" A fine, standard response.

I told my colleague that I'll ask the client, "So, what was it like to eat a bag of chips?" It's a subtle difference, but I hope the impact is clear. I don't invalidate that it felt like a binge, but I work to keep things as objective as possible. We work to investigate before we assign meaning.

I hope I help my clients keep things in perspective. Eating a bag of chips means something only if we let it. To my father, eating a bag of chips means he has to go to the grocery store the next day if he wants more (a regular occurrence). He's never thought this to be "disordered" or a binge. It's nothing more than a Monday evening. He's not distressed. No one has planted a seed that there might be something wrong with enjoying chips. He's living his best life.

I may ask my clients how someone else should feel if they ate a whole bag of chips. The answer I get most often is, "Maybe full, but it's fine. It's not a big deal in the big picture." With this reflection I often say, in jest, that my clients are not special unicorns. That their ideas about how eating can look applies to them just as they think it does for others. They don't like this, but I've found that their distress about it lessens, and without the meaning assigned to something like a whole pizza, there are fewer compensatory actions and it doesn't result in a shame spiral. It moves closer to neutral.

Words mean things, and I find that when I'm clear my clients feel more autonomy and independence in our work. They get to become the experts of their own experience. They don't get emotionally tied to every food decision they make, don't need my constant feedback, and are able to keep the bigger picture in mind. I've received anonymous feedback that I help clients recognize all that was coming through their eating patterns wasn't their fault but was a product of society. I hope my clients know that it doesn't live with them, and their bodies are not the problem.

. . .

I ACKNOWLEDGE MY CLIENTS' SURVIVAL SKILLS FOR WHAT THEY are, and not something that is "disordered," "maladaptive," and/or "behaviors." I help my clients know that however they end up in my office isn't because of their "issues" or their "relationship with their body," though that may be their presenting concern. I hope they see the impacts of societal norms on how they view their eating patterns and their body as narratives that they don't have to keep.

They don't own this; it didn't start with them; this did not happen in a vacuum.

I let them know that the way they have organized their life has worked to mitigate the impacts of white supremacy on their lives. I don't focus on the today-of-things in my practice. My clients and I take a look at all of the individuals who have touched their existence, since they've been alive and in generations past. This includes present-day relationships, and we also walk back centuries and realize that their path to my office makes sense.

We know what happened to Mia.

We know what happened to Lexi.

I got to work with a young woman with an "official" eating disorder diagnosis who had experienced the feelings of being both too much and not enough since childhood. She had taken a break from therapy and her doctor suggested she see a dietitian. The therapist had viewed the client's restriction as the primary problem to be solved, while the client felt that her primary concern was less about her eating patterns and more about lived experience. She didn't think she needed therapy—at this point, it wasn't helpful.

We initially met over Zoom and spent the first couple sessions getting to know each other, and I asked questions about how she views her cultural food. Instead of telling me more about her eating we quickly transitioned to her experience growing up. She was too light-skinned to be considered Brown and too curvy to be white and felt stuck between two cultures. In high school she felt she wasn't getting the attention that she would have received if she had "fit in." After losing a dramatic amount of weight when she moved out on her own, she found that she finally fit. She was getting the attention that she had long desired.

"Soooo, do you feel like you finally fit because you're getting attention from white men now that you don't have curves?"

Her face fell and she took a while to respond.

When she did so, she said, in jest, "I feel like I'm being called out!" and started laughing. "Whooooa. Someone should write a book about that!"

I let her know that I agreed.

I let her know that her experience makes sense. We've been set up to want proximity to whiteness. If I had been focused directly on her eating patterns as the problem, we wouldn't have gotten there. I referred her to a therapist who would focus on her identity development, and unsurprisingly, she started eating meals and snacks and transitioned out of my care.

• • •

I DIDN'T ALWAYS PRACTICE IN THIS WAY.

Early in 2022, Josh was choosing between a therapist whose focus was eating disorders and one who primarily worked with neurodiverse clients. He was doing well with his eating, was flexible with food, and no longer vegan, so I voted for getting primary support with his newly diagnosed ADHD and autism. I also mentioned that I thought keeping connected to eating disorder recovery in some form could be good and perhaps he could find a group for ongoing support. He gave me the same look I'd given him when I was skeptical of what he was telling me. "Oh!" I clarified, "I don't mean one of those 'diet culture is the hardest thing' or 'I'm trying to intuitively eat' groups!"

He laughed. "Those are totally the groups you made me join years ago!" he reminded me.

"Ugh, I knoooooow!" I said. "And I'm so sorry."

Instead, I recommended finding community and friends who shared the same food and body politics, those he could talk to about safety and survival and the intersections of white supremacy and body narratives. And he did.

. . .

THERE ARE FOLKS WHO DO NOT RESONATE WITH MY APPROACH, Black women included. And that's okay. I've met and worked with more than one Black woman who was more comfortable working with an all-white treatment team. Being fully seen is hard in a world that is already exhausting.

"I've recommended that she come back to see you," my colleague told me, "but she says that she can tell that you see right through her, which makes her uncomfortable." My colleague was a white therapist. Our Black eating disorder client preferred to stay working with her instead of having a therapist of color, and was hoping to find a white dietitian. The client was queer and had come out to the therapist, but not to the rest of the treatment team. She just knew that I could see it (I didn't), and feeling seen in her queerness and Blackness was too much for her while trying to eat food. Feelings are hard.

I've consulted for white therapists and dietitians who have Black clients and seek feedback and guidance in their work. Among my suggestions is for the dietitian to ask why the client chose to work with them. When there is an option to see a Black clinician, I'm always curious about why this choice wasn't made. The clinicians and I discuss the complexities for Black women to be fully seen and to carry those narratives into a therapeutic relationship. That it can be easier to think that food- and body-related work is just about eating more and finding "peace" with food and their bodies. I recommend that the clinicians learn how internalized anti-Blackness or other internalized oppression comes through in the way clients view their bodies and eat food. I suggest exploring whom clients feel comfortable sharing this with.

Lexi reviewed a first draft of this book and offered her thoughts on what she would have done if someone had recognized the lengths she was going to make herself smaller. She said, "I think it would be easier for me to see a white dietitian, in some ways, because they would just say 'Yup, you have an [eating disorder]. Here's a three-point plan to fixing it. Byeee.' Or they would say 'Nope, you're good. Keep losing weight. Byeee.' There would be no difficult conversations of what my life actually looks like, no tears rolling down my face about how the world sees me. Just strictly clinical, numbers, stupid BMI chart, and a yes or no. The feelings are the hard part and that's definitely what I shy away from and I don't think that I'm the only one."

We know that she is not the only one.

Feelings are hard.

• • •

THERE IS NOT A MEDICAL OR MENTAL HEALTH DIAGNOSIS FOR centuries of colonialism. There isn't a *DSM* or ICD-10 code for redlining, eminent domain, ableism, cis-het values, anti-fat violence, or internalized anti-Blackness. There isn't a clinical questionnaire that asks whether the patient is a descendant of those who were enslaved. We're not able to hold the complexity of every client with our current medical model and the violence it holds.

Yet clinicians still try. We make assumptions informed by whiteness and we cause harm.

If we need a diagnosis grounded in whiteness in order to support a client or a friend, there's something fundamentally wrong. If clinicians need something grounded in colonialism to validate someone's experience, I believe we have poor clinical skills. Diagnoses lead us to frameworks. What we all know, yet seem to collectively forget, is that these frameworks don't work. If they did, everyone would be healed.

The one thing I'm often prescriptive about with my clients is finding a community of folks with shared identities, online or in person. I ask my clients to build new relationships with those who share values about eating and bodies. I push people to see parts of their identities reflected in others, something that I've found is often lacking for people who have largely been isolated. I strongly believe in community care and find that those connections do much more to support my clients in their newly discovered identities and/or politics than I will ever be able to. I recommend books like *Belly of the Beast, Thick, Heavy, Fearing the Black Body, Fattily Ever After, #VERYFAT #VERYBRAVE, Pleasure Activism, Revenge Body,* the limited series podcast *My Black Body Podcast,* the podcast *Unsolicited: Fatties Talk Back,* organizations like NOLOSE, many social media accounts, and events like Cupcakes and Muffintops, a plus-size clothing and bake sale held annually in the Bay Area. I also recognize my limitations and refer clients to colleagues who share their identities and/or bring in colleagues to supplement our work.

Body-related vulnerability can be terrifying, especially when traditional therapies are steeped in whiteness. It makes sense that many of us might not be ready.

. . .

REWRITING VULNERABILITY FOR BLACK WOMEN COULD MEAN that we're able to reclaim some of the agency lost when we're assigned special alien status by society. We deserve to live full, complex, and complicated lives. As much as we need voting rights, free health care, and free therapy, we deserve joy, softness, and pleasure. As much as we need destruction of the school-to-prison pipeline, we need destruction of the resilient, impenetrable Black woman archetype. We deserve vulnerability.

I know this to be true, yet working two full-time jobs and determined to push through my seizures without asking for help while writing this book, I wasn't sure what vulnerability looked like in practice.

I went to the primary popular source, Brené Brown. I watched her TED Talk "The Power of Vulnerability" to learn more. She tells the audience that when we numb, we numb all of our feelings:

> We live in a vulnerable world. And one of the ways we deal with it is we numb vulnerability.
>
> And I think there's evidence—and it's not the only reason this evidence exists, but I think it's a huge cause. We are the most in

debt, obese, addicted, and medicated adult cohort in US history. The problem is—and I learned this from the research—that you cannot selectively numb emotion. You can't say, "Here's the bad stuff. Here's vulnerability, here's grief, here's shame, here's fear, here's disappointment. I don't want to feel these, I'm going to have a couple of beers and a banana nut muffin." And it becomes this dangerous cycle.[2]

I understand the overall message she is trying to communicate, but her synopsis was deeply classist, ableist, fatphobic, and did not resonate. But I continued watching. At minute 18:59, she says that the path to vulnerability is "to let ourselves be seen, deeply seen, vulnerably seen." She tells us to "practice gratitude and joy in those moments of terror" and think that "I'm just so grateful, because to feel this vulnerable means I'm alive."[3]

I sat with the message and asked myself if what I want from being vulnerable in this world is to be seen.

I do not.

When I'm talking to colleagues and supervisors about how we need to do better for our marginalized clients, they are seeing me. They are watching as I give away pieces of myself to make the case that our clients deserve more. When I'm setting boundaries with non-Black colleagues and friends, I'm letting myself be seen. When I'm speaking at conferences and deviating from what is acceptable and palatable, I'm seen. To be seen is not what I'm looking for. I'm already hypervisible in most situations. People turn their heads when I walk into a store or sit down at their boardroom table. Being seen, vulnerably seen, all of the time is exhausting.

This wasn't what I was looking for in my search to apply vulnerability to the experiences of Black women who are assigned resilience from birth.

I want to be vulnerable by default. To be an average individual in a world, profession, and field that are determined to remind me that I'm only here because of luck and that I need to be grateful for the opportunity, even if it . . . isn't.

I don't want to be expected to give 100 percent of my focus and attention to my professional life. I'm no math nerd, but it seems like constantly giving 100 percent to my work means that certain areas of my life will receive 0 percent. I want vulnerability to mean that I am afforded the same opportunity to be average, or even just good at my job as my less melanated coworkers are without critique of "lacking work ethic." I want to be expected to reserve some of myself for my family, friends, and community as we are all pushing back against white supremacy and capitalism.

I don't want to be expected to go "above and beyond" to support my non-Black peers and colleagues. I don't want to be mammified by my superiors. I don't want my friends and me to be tone policed and expected to take a gentler, coddling approach. I don't want to have my direct, brief statements be interpreted as angry and confrontational rather than concise and clear.

Brown's website states that this is "the bottom line: I believe that you have to walk through vulnerability to get to courage, therefore . . . embrace the suck. I try to be grateful every day, and my motto right now is 'Courage over comfort.'"[4]

Black women are inherently courageous. I want for us to be rewritten as vulnerable rather than assigned resilience. I want for us to have comfort and ease.

Brown's work wasn't for me, so I went to the googles and typed in: "Black woman vulnerable" and eight out of ten of the top results were about Black women and their vulnerability to physical harm and assault. Of course. We will always be examined and studied for our trauma and susceptibility to violence, not for our capacity to feel something other than our pain.

This made sense after I looked up the Merriam-Webster's definition of the word.

ESSENTIAL MEANING OF *VULNERABLE*

1. easily hurt or harmed physically, mentally, or emotionally
2. open to attack, harm, or damage

The American Psychological Association defines vulnerability similarly:

1. *n.* susceptibility to developing a condition, disorder, or disease when exposed to specific agents or conditions.—vulnerable *adj.*

These definitions of vulnerability aren't working for me as the antidote to being assigned impenetrability. I don't see myself or my friends in them.

I'd like to rewrite part of the story of vulnerability, for myself and my loved ones. To add definitions to the word in ways that allow for possibility and are not grounded in pain and trauma.

How about:

NEW MEANING OF *VULNERABLE*

1. access to a full range of emotions and experiences

2. embodied softness

3. the ability to just *be*

"There's something in yearning for . . . freedom that's both collective and people get to . . . just be fully self-expressed." Shana, Fresh, Ifasina, and I were discussing the realities of being seen as a monolith and the ways that some Black folks view others' actions as a reflection of themselves; this was Fresh's vision for freedom. We talked about how this can create constant tension in ourselves and among ourselves. That it's exhausting. We discussed the opportunity to be seen for the individuals we are. "Man, that seems like the life, right? Where you could just be yourself. You can, just, be." Fresh shared a whole word.

• • •

I JUST PASSED THE FORTY-YEAR MARK. I'M NOT GOING TO LIVE forever, especially if I continue to work among those who mammify me and treat me as something to be feared or just discard me. Going forward, I need to do things differently. In this new chapter of my life, I'd like to invest in a new flavor of joy. I want to just *be*. I don't want to be a special alien; I want to be basic.

Basictivity is a word I need. A cozy-sounding noun that will find a home in the Urban Dictionary. Doesn't it offer ease? It's warm, just like the pumpkin spice scented candles that I would light in the fall and place next to my tiny pumpkins. Basictivity sounds comfy, like the fuzzy socks that I would wear as I shuffle across my gray, laminate flooring to get to my Keurig cups.

Being basic would mean that I could relax and wouldn't have to be aware of my surroundings at all times. I wouldn't have to justify my actions, my existence, or how I ended up in the same room with a bunch of white folks who weren't prepared for a Black woman to Know Something.

I want to get out of bed in the morning and gather 87 percent of my tousled hair into a hair band, throw on my lululemon leggings and UGGs on the way to my doctor appointment. When I get there, I want to be trusted when I describe what's happening with my own body. Thinking about what to wear to appointments during which I need to be believed and heard is standard issue. Walking in looking like I just left a yoga class is my kinda comfort; I want that life.

When climate change makes California uninhabitable, I want to choose my next neighborhood in a new state to be chosen based on its proximity to a Chipotle or Trader Joe's. I would rather skip the analysis of whether my dad might be shot by the police officer called to my home after a neighbor sees a "suspicious person" lurking in *their* neighborhood. Oh, and while I'm house hunting, let's shoot for the moon! I want to meet with any realtor and expect they will show me all of the houses in my price range rather than only those from the areas for which I would be a "good fit." I'll fly to my next neighborhood wearing leggings, Crocs, a personalized necklace with my name spelled out in gold, and a bonnet on my head. I'm not here to perform.

I want to move into my ranch-style home and head right out to grab some necessities. Of course, I'll hit up the nearby Target, which I will call Targé without any sense of irony. I look forward to buying distressed wooden signs for said new home that say things like LIVE,

LAUGH, LOVE, canvas prints that say YOU'RE DOING THE BEST YOU CAN, and corrugated metal letters attached to wood that say WELCOME to adorn my lavender-painted accent wall and to hang next to the string art of my new state with a red heart over my new city.

I can't wait to walk into West Elm and buy my midcentury modern furniture. The employees will greet me enthusiastically, and not with the direction to "please check your bag at the counter, ma'am," when every other Susan in there has her purse. Oh no, they will want to help me find what I need and assume I have the money to buy it!

I want to demonstrate my wokeness to the new neighbors with signs on my lawn that say things like IN THIS HOUSE WE BELIEVE SCIENCE IS REAL, and I will forever keep my COEXIST bumper sticker.

When I update my neighborhood Facebook profile info with my new location, I'll also be sure to change my cover image to one that proclaims "Silence is Violence!" and then never, ever say anything that could be construed as "too political." I'm going for ease, and my new neighbor Karen might get defensive about her whiteness if I had the audacity to share my own experience of Blackness. I don't need her putting white supremacy, privilege, or microaggression in confusing "quotations." Oh no, the status quo is my new playground.

When I sit down to write in my new home office, I want to write books about my life that tell women it's as easy as washing your face and not apologizing (girl). I want to use my basic life as an example of how to Do Hard Things. It would be great if I could actually see myself in books like those and truly believe that I can "dare greatly."[5]

I'll look to my left, at the wall I painted with chalkboard paint. It will have my Basic Bish Bucket List on it, which will include buying Yitty shapewear for the next Taylor Swift concert.

At the top of the list I will have goals like getting white girl wasted, which, oddly enough, my dad will be able to help me with. He makes an adult beverage that I can only describe as sorority inspired. He fills up a thrift store glass with ice and then pours boxed red wine halfway up the glass and tops it off with Canada Dry ginger ale. My pops sips this during the summer evenings. He calls it a wine cooler; I call it iconic.

I'll start a Basic Bish blog and chronicle my easeful evenings spent with friends under my pergola, drinking frosé from plastic wine glasses in my backyard. I won't have to worry about a neighbor calling the cops for a noise complaint while we laugh and play music.

It really does sound simple, doesn't it?

To just *be*.

• • •

LEXI IS REWRITING HER STORY. AND SHE DIDN'T EVEN NOTICE.

When she visited us for the holiday season in 2021, to work at a nearby veterinary clinic and celebrate with us, she was surprised to find that she hadn't left her flat iron here from her previous stay. She didn't buy another one for the entire month. Instead, she braided her hair after washing it and left it somewhat wavy when she wore it down.

At the end of her stay, I asked her about her hair, and she told me, "Eh, I always pull my hair up when I go to work anyhow." Which is true. Though the first time she stayed with us she would warn us before she straightened her hair before work because the small house would smell like burning hair. She'd often talk to a friend on the phone while pulling her hair through the flat iron over and over. And then she'd gather it into a bun for work.

I never brought up that on the podcast episode we recorded together she talked about straightening her hair in the UK before going to work.

During the recording, she surprised me by saying that someday she wants to explore living unapologetically.

"So one of these days . . . gradually, I will be lighting the world on fire and just letting it happen," she said.

I've seen the sparks, and it makes me hopeful for the future.

I hope one day this world will be able to rewrite itself to be one in which Black women can live unapologetically and just *be*.

chapter ten

Celebrate Black Joy

S ONYA RENEE TAYLOR IS A BRILLIANT BLACK POET, WRITER,
educator, and activist. In 2020, she let us know that she had decided to be her "own gift giver. To lavish myself with delights. To
do some extravagant BAWSE shit unapologetically. To live into my
Decadence practice as a reminder not to wait for this raggedy place
to treat me with care. I'd better get to doing it myself. I cannot be
told a GOT DAMN THANG in this joint. Won't you celebrate with
me that every day 2020 has tried to kill me and has failed." She
posted a photo of herself leaning against her new car and informed
her followers, "PS if you fix your lips to share anything but joy on
this post today you will get cussed the fuck out. I'm not your guru.
Not your mammy or your mule. I'm not a brand. I'm a whole ass
human being who will not be kind to attempts to shrink me, shame

me, or belittle me for how I show myself care and love." And yet the haters still came for her, of course, shaming her for the ways that she finds joy, even for participating in capitalism at all. And she noticed her "instinct to acquiesce" to the white people interrogating and shaming her for her joy.

Black Joy is resistance in a world that views Black women as valuable for our labor, only. Sonya deserves to be celebrated for her joy. We all do.

• • •

"HEADSHOTS AND JOYSHOTS!" READ THE SUBJECT HEADING OF MY email.

In spring of 2022, I was heading down to LA to visit Alison for our first IRL "post"-COVID meetup before she packed up her city life and moved to the country and figured that LA would be a good place to get headshot photos taken. I'd had professional photos taken in the past, but all of them had washed out my skin color and given it a sickly glow. It wasn't until talking with folks in the entertainment industry that I learned having the appropriate lighting equipment and photography skills to capture all the melanin that darker skin has to offer is not standard practice, and in fact has been used as a "reason" to not cast darker-skinned characters next to their pale peers. Of course.

I not only wanted a photo, I wanted one of me smiling, teeth out and looking happy, jolly, laughing even. I had approximately zero names of photographers and no ideas for how to find one; a Yelp search seemed like not the best plan. Instead, I worked backward. I thought about joy, then who I've seen radiate joy, then who is Black—and of course came up with Nicole Byer. She is joy goals for me. Sequins, sparkles, bright colors, big laughs, big smiles, and plush shark slippers. I grabbed her book off the shelf, looked at the name of the photographer and googled her. Kim Newmoney's portfolio was everything I wanted to see. She has well-lit people of all skin tones and people of all sizes featured prominently. The thought of doing anything alone in LA makes me anxious, so I talked Shana into coming with me.

Kim has some pretty famous folks, including Byer, on her website. I think I was sweating when I emailed her on a Wednesday morning. I told her how I found her and how important capturing Nicole Byer's joy had meant to many. I asked her if she could take some joyful headshots—joyshots!—of me and Shana. It felt like a long shot, but I'd never know unless I asked. In the approx thirty hours that followed, I asked around for any additional photographer recommendations folks had because I was sure I'd never hear from Kim. I remember getting her reply the next day and writing multiple texts in all caps to my friends: *SHE ACTUALLY REPLIED!!* Granted, this was just a reply with a fee schedule, no availability discussed or anything scheduled, but I didn't care. I was one step closer to her taking my picture! I replied immediately with availability and somehow managed to wait six days without hearing back before I checked in with her. After a couple more emails back and forth, we were able to confirm a date. Oh-Em-Geeeee!

The day before the shoot, we arrived at Alison's house. She had voluntarily washed her legs to mark our visit; I was touched. Shana and I hopped on a call with Kim after I got some language pointers from Alison and Shana: *author photo*, *book jacket*, and *editorial photos* (got it). Kim was lovely, very much wanting to support our vision. Shana was looking for a professionally whimsical feel and I was looking for professionally joyful. Shana and I decided to take some pics together for any collaborative future endeavors. The call was epically LA. Kim sprinkled "vibes" throughout the chat; I loved it. It put my LA-specific anxiety at ease. I feel strongly that it's a city that requires a secret decoder ring to navigate. She assured me it would be chill: "It's all vibes."

After the call, Shana, Alison, Alison's kiddo, and I grabbed buckwheat pancakes, eggs, and rose lemonade. Shana and I got to hear more about the work Alison and other community members in the entertainment industry were doing to make safer experiences for performers and crew members in the film and television industry.

After I finished my food and the rest of Shana's, we all stopped by a shop that offers items for living a magical life before walking across the street to the Plus Bus Boutique. Shana and I picked out a variety of items, with some expert styling from Alison's kiddo and the shop stylist. We each left with a couple clothes and accessories that made us even more camera ready. It was all vibes.

At noon the next day, we pulled up to the studio and got to getting all dolled up. We pulled out our four different outfits and immediately realized that we'd each gotten an outfit from the Plus Bus of the same exact color. Mine was a sequined top (of course), and Shana's was an adorable shorts jumpsuit; they gave sparkly and whimsy. It was destined to be a great day.

We danced to nineties hip-hop and Lizzo while we each vogued for the camera off and on for the next six hours. Kim was the greatest. Nothing could kill our vibes—not even the random white dude who decided to barge into the studio five seconds after learning that there were Black women inside to tell us we were having too much fun and needed to turn the music down for his Zoom call. Nope, not today, Brad.

We wrapped up and I thanked Kim multiple times, mostly for her work, but also for quelling my anxiety enough for me to have a good time. I may or may not have lowkey asked her if she wanted to be my friend someday. Shana enjoyed watching my not-so-subtle standom.

Later that month we got the proofs back and saw that our Black Joy was perfectly captured. You can see for yourself; Shana is the model on the cover of this book; she radiates joy and light. At the back of the book you will find a photo of me from that day.

We will rewrite the narrative of Blackness that centers and celebrates our joy.

· · ·

WE ALL DESERVE TO HAVE JOY CENTERED IN CONVERSATIONS about bodies. To center pleasure and laughter when living. I want a version of a "lifestyle brand" that centers joy instead of Health, Wellness, or guardrails. I want one that doesn't ignore that life is really fucking hard sometimes, and doesn't tell us to just choose happiness, though encourages us to access joy when possible. A balance of reality and aspiration. I could get into it.

Actually, I'll get into it. This company will offer candles, ones we can light to set the mood. I'll offer a "Smells Like My Joy" candle. It will have hints of cedar, smoke, and evergreen, with green and pink glitter to evoke a frolic in the woods. Another joytime candle will have notes of orange, clove, and red wine; it is always a good time for sangria. The "Smells Like My Meltdown" candle will have hints of musk (of course) along with some eucalyptus from my goat's-milk soap and lavender from my "natural" deodorant. I will invite folks to light it when experiencing a meltdown of their own. Suffering in solitude can be isolating but knowing that someone else has wondered "WTF am I *even doing*?!" while being a blubbering mess could bring a sense of comfort.

I can see this company doing well.

I will take contributions from laypeople and professionals alike who could offer their "Top 5 Places to Travel Safely While Black," "Top 5 Plants That Won't Die If You Forget to Water Them for a Month Because Depression and the Hustle Are REAL," and "Top 5 Foods for Eating Your Feelings."

The company will offer playlists for mentally preparing to endure another anti-racism "training" with your mostly white coworkers. We will also offer a Juneteenth-inspired playlist curated by old Black folks and one from everyone's favorite aunties.

How could this brand not offer a Dust?! We all need Unicorn Dust, collected from unicorn dander and enhanced with some natural unicorn glitter. When we mix it into coffee, tea, or bubbly water and drink it, it will transport us to the last moment we experienced pure joy and take us away from whatever garbage fire is unfolding around us. I need this. Now.

I could pay journalists to find the answers to hard questions like, "What are key strategies for cultural revolution?" I'd also like to know: Who ate one-seventh of a donut in the breakroom and put the rest back?!

I love a good novelty item. This lifestyle brand will include some petty items; what company wouldn't? I'll offer Leg Soap for white people, a bar of soap with activated charcoal so that it exfoliates the skin without someone needing to bother with a loofah or wash-cloth. It will be scented with patchouli. Of course it will.

I also see a market for the white tears that Black women are regularly subjected to. Why let them go to waste? The brand will offer tiny little packets of calcium, magnesium, potassium, flavor-ing, and some sugar to mix with the collected salty tears and trans-form them into a hydration beverage. I can use them while I seek out groups like Outdoor Afro and Black and Camping once my company is off the ground.

I'll also offer a starter seasoning pack for those just easing into the concept of flavoring their food. The first container in the pack would be empty, to be used to build up the muscles in one's wrist that shaking seasoning requires.

I will commission Netflix documentaries on the many, many beautiful ways there are to be Black, and another on honoring Black Joy and the various ways we wield it as the weapon it is.

We all deserve an app with various recordings of laughs that are as big and unapologetic as Crissle West's, from *The Read* podcast, that we could play, loudly, anytime. It could be used to pump us up, to give the feeling that we're experiencing joy with someone else, and especially when someone in public has just given us the side eye for a slight chuckle.

The peak of this company's offerings would be a Tab Collab. We'd create a software workaround so that Tabitha Brown's soul-ful and soothing voice could be an option for all mapping apps, Siri, Alexa, and every automatic recording we have to sit through in order to simply speak with a representative. Hearing her say "Hello there" when we need directions, want to play the newest Jazmine

Sullivan album, or set an alarm would bring light to any day. Listening to her tell us that it is on her spirit to reroute us after a wrong turn would have us arriving everywhere feeling cool, calm, and collected.

We deserve joy.

• • •

WHITNEY, MY WORK WIFE, FINDS JOY IN HER HUSBAND AND daughter, being in authentic community, walking, and getting her nails done.

Alishia finds joy in drawing, writing poetry, creating playlists, eating a delicious meal, having a nourishing conversation with someone, consuming plant medicine, watching Black-ass shows, tending to her plants, reading books from the wisdom of Black feminists, being at her ancestral altar, having a good time with Black kin, sitting out in the sun on a warm and breezy afternoon, going to Black- and Brown-centered countries, listening to the sound of birds, watching the wind flow through the trees, and spending time by the ocean and saltwater.

One of the friends mentioned in this book enjoys making and drinking wine slushies, hiking, orgasms, and travel. She finds joy in sporting a crop top and in the functionality of leggings with pockets. She loves a good cookout.

Outside of cooking, Fresh is a sex-positive fat activist, lover of hip-hop, tiny homes, riding their bike ridiculously long distances, and growing their own food.

Ifasina finds joy in dance. They create and hold digital and remote fat-centered dance classes, workshops, and creative programs through their creative project called Get Embodied Soul Movement. Ifasina says, "I center and actively interrogate systemic ableism, infantilization of Disabled people, and my own internalized ableism." Their work also "actively interrogate[s] systemic sizeism, healthism, and body fascism and [their] own internalized anti-fat bias." "I dance because I am. Because I am, I dance."

Shana finds joy in walking into a warm ocean with her clothes still on, reading really fun banter in a romance novel, eating French pastries, and watching *The Courtship* with her sister while drinking wine. She also finds joy in having her hair oiled, watching her niece eat ice cream, and eating Butterfinger Blizzards from Dairy Queen.

Lexi loves a grilled cheese with grilled onions and green chiles and fries from In-N-Out; it's her number one request after we pick her up at the airport. Since being in the UK, she has found lots of joy traveling to new countries she chooses by typing "flights from London from 15 pounds." She also finds joy in watermelon-flavored Sour Patch Kids, white cheddar Cheez-Its (as you know). Her favorite escape after a long day is watching trash TV; her analyses of the dynamics at play are impressive. She also enjoys trying to convince me cats are better than dogs, yet has failed up to this point.

I find joy in dancing and singing at the top of my lungs, regardless of whether I know the words. I love dogs, especially my overly anxious but lovable pair. I find joy in recalling memories while scrolling through my phone looking at the many photographs I've taken over the years. Garden competitions with my dad are contentious but enjoyable nonetheless and watching him garden with a Backwoods cigar hanging out of his mouth will always make me laugh. Dirt is amazing; I like to camp in it, hike over it, and frolic across it. I will never get tired of people watching, especially at queer dance clubs, gay brunches, and dive bars. I *love* wearing clothes and makeup that sparkle and shimmer, all day, every day. I could eat eggs for multiple meals in a day and enjoy chips and donuts for pleasure. I adore the quirky mishmash of people who end up on *Nailed It!* and Nicole Byer's epic outfits on the show. Listening to a group of Black women laughing loudly will almost always bring me to tears.

Black Joy is beautiful.

Black Joy is everything.

It deserves to be recognized and celebrated for the resistance it is.

Black Joy is a weapon for us to wield in a world constantly trying to deny us our humanity.

The narratives of Black women are being rewritten to center our joy.

Joy has always been ours.

Acknowledgments

*T*HIS BOOK WAS WRITTEN ON UNCEDED INDIGENOUS MIWOK AND *Nisenan land in the area of California now called Sacramento. The Wilton Rancheria is the only federally recognized Indigenous tribe in the Sacramento area. The members "are descendants of the Penutian linguistic family identified as speaking the Miwok dialect" (https://wiltonrancheria -nsn.gov/).*

As you've witnessed on these pages, this book was far from a solo effort. I'm so grateful for the many thinkers, leaders, and friends who have touched this project. I am a deeply relational person and I would be nothing without the amazing people around me.

Lexi, I will condense my love and gratitude and simply say thank you for being you. This book is for you and all others whose self-harm was normalized and celebrated. Your trust in me to hold your story means more than you will ever know. "What are you going to do about it?" is both the best and hardest question that you ask me. Your faith that I will make a good decision and your belief that I can create social change are what keep me going. I can't wait for you to light it all on fire and see what happens!

To my spouse: I cherish your empathy. You saw someone being brave and vulnerable and thought that I might be able to support her; this forever changed us all. Thank you for asking me to show up for Lexi that day, and thank you for always showing up for me. You held things down while I worked two full-time jobs and never stopped believing in me or this book. I love you infinity.

Shana, my lit(erary) friend. Your presence in this book and in my life will be forever cherished. I'm so grateful for your friendship, your trust, and your willingness to get donuts and listen to all of my writing meltdowns. You have the best laugh and everyone deserves to hear it, loudly, in public. You and Lexi read this book in its earliest draft and both of you made it better; you both make me better every day!

Ifasina, your ancestors shine through you and you light up the world with your love and light. Your capacity to hold the complexities of all of humanity is a gift you do not take lightly; we see you. Your presence in my life has been grounding over the years and I'm so grateful for your friendship. Fresh, your wisdom radiates from within. Your relationship with land is beautiful and vibrates through the healing your craft provides. I am incredibly honored that you both shared your stories for this audience. I wish for so much levity in your lives and hope we can get together with Shana to laugh loudly and play sometime soon!

Dad, thanks for providing the signature cocktail for my book. You taught me the power that comes when we say "fuck it" and decide to build our own table. The way you have structured your workday around your afternoon nap is my primary self-employment goal. I'm so grateful that the connection to the earth that our ancestors forged has passed on to me, and that it's something we get to share. Thanks for teaching me how to eat food.

Amy, I couldn't have managed this pandemic and writing process without our text chats with topics about Blackness and bodies that were debated for days. Rolling out the butcher paper across the outdoor patio floor with you was an essential brainstorming method that I hope to continue. You will forever be the best travel planner I know.

Natalie, somehow you said yes to going to Goop while pregnant, something I will forever be grateful for. Thank you for our weekly video chats during COVID; they provided some semblance of a beginning and end to a week among days at home that stretched to eternity. I appreciate your willingness to hold my Big Feelings throughout this process. You will be the first to get a Smells Like My Meltdown candle.

To all of my rad Black colleagues in the field, particularly the kinfolk. Whitney, Alishia, Angela, Safiya, Brianna, and all the rest, thanks for assuring me that this book is important to the field and to Black women. You are the colleagues I was waiting for.

Thanks to everyone involved with supporting and producing *My Black Body Podcast* and telling the stories of Black bodies.

Thanks to my mother for her unwavering support.

Renee, you somehow convinced and then trusted me to transform fifty-word captions into a sixty-five-thousand-word book. I'm still very unclear how it happened. Thank you. And thanks to Hachette Go for supporting this project.

Tanya and Carol at McKinnon Literary, thanks so much for believing in this message.

Thanks to all of my clients, especially those within these pages, for trusting me with your body stories.

Lastly, thanks to Black women everywhere for simply existing. Your body stories are yours to own.

Notes

INTRODUCTION

1. Isabel Wilkerson, *Caste: The Origins of Our Discontents* (New York: Random House, 2020), 17.

2. Angela Meadows and Sigrún Daníelsdóttir, "What's in a Word? On Weight Stigma and Terminology," *Frontiers in Psychology* 7 (2016): 1527, https://doi.org/10.3389/fpsyg.2016.01527.

3. Ashleigh Shackelford, "Fat Is Not a Bad Word," *Teen Vogue*, August 26, 2019, https://www.teenvogue.com/story/fat-is-not-a-bad-word.

4. Da'Shaun L. Harrison, *Belly of the Beast: The Politics of Anti-Fatness as Anti-Blackness* (Berkeley: North Atlantic Books, 2021), 107.

CHAPTER 1: IT ISN'T DIET CULTURE, IT'S WHITE SUPREMACY

1. Justin Parkinson, "The Significance of Sarah Baartman," *BBC News Magazine*, January 7, 2016, https://www.bbc.com/news/magazine-35240987.

2. Sabrina Strings, *Fearing the Black Body: The Racial Origins of Fat Phobia* (New York: New York University Press, 2019), 89.

3. Christy Harrison, *Anti-Diet: Reclaim Your time, Money, Well-Being, and Happiness Through Intuitive Eating* (New York: Little, Brown Spark, 2019), 4.

4. Jes Baker, "Why I've Chosen Body Liberation Over Body Love," Jes Baker, https://www.jesbaker.com/why-body-liberation.

CHAPTER 2: SPECIAL ALIENS WHO CAN HEAL THE WORLD!: RESILIENCE

1. Marianne Schnall, "When Black Women Lead, We All Win," *Forbes*, August 19, 2020, https://www.forbes.com/sites/marianneschnall/2020/08/17/when-black-women-lead-we-all-win/?sh=529e5bc14513.

2. Kate Bolduan, "Black Women Are the Backbone of the Democratic Party. And They Feel the Heavy Burden of This Election," CNN, October 21, 2020, https://www.cnn.com/2020/10/21/politics/black-women-voters-michigan/index.html.

3. Bolduan, "Black Women Are the Backbone."

4. Isabel Wilkerson, *Caste: The Origins of Our Discontents* (New York: Random House, 2020), 141.

5. "The Sapphire Caricature," Ferris State University, Jim Crow Museum, https://www.ferris.edu/HTMLS/news/jimcrow/antiblack/sapphire.htm.

6. "The Jezebel Stereotype," Ferris State University, Jim Crow Museum, https://www.ferris.edu/HTMLS/news/jimcrow/jezebel/index.htm.

7. Gabriella Paiella, "Wait, What: The Week in 'WAP,'" *GQ*, August 14, 2020, https://www.gq.com/story/the-week-in-wap.

8. C. Vernon Coleman II, "Snoop Dogg Doesn't Agree with Cardi B's 'Wap,' Encourages Women to Have Privacy and Leave Things to the Imagination," *XXL*, December 12, 2020, https://www.xxlmag.com/snoop-dogg-doesnt-agree-cardi-b-wap/.

9. Jordan Schnitzer Family Foundation, *Beyond Mammy, Jezebel & Sapphire: Reclaiming Images of Black Women* (catalog of exhibit at Alexandria Museum of Art, Alexandria, LA, from December 2, 2016, to February 18, 2017,

and at IDEA Space at Colorado College, Colorado Springs, CO, from March 27 to May 10, 2017) (Portland, OR: Jordan Schnitzer Family Foundation, 2016), 18.

10. Ronald G. Shafer, "Hattie McDaniel Was the First Black Oscar Winner. It Didn't Help Her Career," *Washington Post*, March 27, 2022, https://www.washingtonpost.com/history/2022/03/27/hattie-mcdaniel-academy-award/.

11. Jessie W. Parkhurst, "The Role of the Black Mammy in the Plantation Household," *Journal of Negro History* 23, no. 5 (July 1938): 356, https://www.journals.uchicago.edu/doi/10.2307/2714687.

12. Jessica Lim, "The Hate on Simone Biles Is Everything That Is Wrong with Society," *Medium*, July 29, 2021, https://medium.com/@jessicalim/the-hate-on-simone-biles-is-everything-that-is-wrong-with-society-e2a1a78f2b85.

13. "I Am Simone," episode 7, *Simone vs Herself*, September 28, 2021, https://www.facebook.com/2074347926132282/videos/980381319196818?__so__=watchlist&__rv__=video_home_www_playlist_video_list.

14. Camonghne Felix, "Simone Biles Chose Herself: 'I Should Have Quit Way Before Tokyo,'" *The Cut*, September 27, 2021, https://www.thecut.com/article/simone-biles-olympics-2021.html.

15. Simone Biles, "I've pushed through so much the past couple years," Instagram post, September 4, 2021, https://www.instagram.com/p/CTZ_ph6HV_u/?utm_source=ig_embed&ig_rid=37bb9a0c-791f-455c-8ee2-8c13acda6b07.

16. Michael D. Shear, "Biden Made a Campaign Pledge to Put a Black Woman on the Supreme Court," *New York Times*, January 26, 2022, https://www.nytimes.com/2022/01/26/us/politics/biden-supreme-court-black-woman.html.

17. Jennifer Chudy and Hakeem Jefferson, "Support for Black Lives Matter Surged Last Year. Did It Last?" *New York Times*, May 22, 2021, https://www.nytimes.com/2021/05/22/opinion/blm-movement-protests-support.html.

18. Marco Quiroz-Gutierrez, "American Companies Pledged $50 Billion to Black Communities. Most of It Hasn't Materialized," *Fortune*, May 6,

2021, https://fortune.com/2021/05/06/us-companies-black-communities
-money-50-billion/.

CHAPTER 3: "FOR OUR OWN GOOD": RESPECTABILITY

1. Mo'Nique (@therealmoworldwide), "Represent Yourself with Pride," Instagram video, May 21, 2021, https://www.instagram.com/p/CPdqpiSh-TZ/.

2. Gene Demby, Shereen Marisol Meraji, Karen Grigsby Bates, Alyssa Jeong Perry, and Leah Donnella, "Code Switch: What's in a 'Karen'?" *It's Been a Minute* (podcast), NPR, August 4, 2020, https://www.npr.org/2020/07/27/895990398/code-switch-whats-in-a-karen.

3. Shereen Marisol Meraji and Gene Demby, "The Racial Reckoning That Wasn't," *Code Switch* (podcast), NPR, June 9, 2021, https://www.npr.org/transcripts/1004467239.

4. Crystal, "177: Jenn Sherman's Yacht Rock Ride Removed and Our Interview with Jenny Westin," *The Clipout*, October 9, 2020, https://www.thecolipout.com/177-jenn-shermans-yacht-rock-ride-removed-and-our-interview-with-jenny-westin/.

5. Mikaela Pitcan, Alice E. Marwick, and danah boyd, "Performing a Vanilla Self: Respectability Politics, Social Class, and the Digital World," *Journal of Computer-Mediated Communication* 23, no. 3 (May 2018): 163–179, https://doi.org/10.1093/jcmc/zmy008.

6. Paisley Jane Harris, "Gatekeeping and Remaking: The Politics of Respectability in African American Women's History and Black Feminism," *Journal of Women's History* 15, no. 1 (2003): 212–220, https://doi.org/10.1353/jowh.2003.0025.

7. Home page, NOLOSE, https://nolose.org/.

CHAPTER 4: TOO MUCH, YET NOT ENOUGH: RESTRICTION

1. Frank Deford, "Nadia Awed Ya: Everybody Flipped Over the 14-Year-Old Nadia Comaneci, as She Made Gymnastics Look Like Child's Play and Scored Seven 10s," *Sports Illustrated*, August 2, 1976, https://vault.si.com/vault/1976/08/02/nadia-comaneci-1976-olympics-perfect-scores.

2. Maryann Hudson, "A Balanced Personality: National Gymnastics Champion Dominique Dawes Does Not Allow Herself to Be Easily Ruffled," *Los Angeles Times*, March 4, 1995, https://www.latimes.com/archives/la-xpm-1995-03-04-sp-38695-story.html.

3. Elaine Welteroth, "August Cover Star Gabby Douglas Is Determined to Make Olympic History Again. She's Going for Gold," *Teen Vogue*, June 30, 2016, https://www.teenvogue.com/story/gabby-douglas-summer-olympics-cover-august-2016.

4. Rebecca Epstein, Jamilia J. Blake, and Thalia González, *Girlhood Interrupted: The Erasure of Black Girls' Childhood* (Washington, DC: Georgetown Law, Center on Poverty and Inequality), https://genderjusticeandopportunity.georgetown.edu/wp-content/uploads/2020/06/girlhood-interrupted.pdf.

5. Over the years, people have re-created these questions for their own handouts; these are a direct quote from the one given to me.

6. Alexis Brown (@lexi_sbrown), "I was called up as first place," Instagram post, June 4, 2020, https://www.instagram.com/p/CBBcmG7JAOV/.

7. Lasse Bang, Øyvind Rø, and Tor Endestad, "Normal Gray Matter Volumes in Women Recovered from Anorexia Nervosa: A Voxel-Based Morphometry Study," *BMC Psychiatry* 16 (2016): 144, https://doi.org/10.1186/s12888-016-0856-z.

CHAPTER 5: FEELING GOOD AS HELL: BODY TOXITIVITY

1. Brittany Spanos, "The Joy of Lizzo: She Has Become a New Kind of Pop Superstar, Full of Relentless Positivity. But It Took a Long Time and a Lot of Heartache," *Rolling Stone*, January 22, 2020, https://www.rollingstone.com/music/music-features/lizzo-cover-story-interview-truth-hurts-grammys-937009/.

2. Jenna Amatulli, "Lizzo Responds to Backlash After Sharing Juice Cleanse with Fans," *HuffPost*, December 15, 2020, https://www.huffpost.com/entry/lizzo-body-positivity-juice-detox_n_5fd8f70dc5b663c3759a5424.

3. Lizzo (lizzobeeating), Instagram, December 15, 2020, https://www.instagram.com/p/CI1IItHBX58/?hl=en.

4. Shyla Watson, "Lizzo Wore an NSFW Outfit to a Basketball Game and It Sparked a Debate About Body Type Double Standards," *Buzzfeed*, December 9, 2020, https://www.buzzfeed.com/shylawatson/lizzo-laker-game-outfit-twitter-debate.

5. Daily Blast LIVE, "Lizzo Twerks in Thong at LA Lakers Game," YouTube video, 2:38, December 9, 2019, https://www.youtube.com/watch?app=desktop&v=2vPpEQRYrvw.

6. Home page, Body Project, https://thebodypositive.org.

7. A. C. Ciao, B. R. Munson, K. D. Pringle, S. R. Roberts, L. A. Lalgee, K. A. Lawley, and J. Brewster, "Inclusive Dissonance-Based Body Image Interventions for College Students: Two Randomized-Controlled Trials of the EVERYbody Project," *Journal of Consulting and Clinical Psychology* 89, no. 4 (2021): 301–315, https://doi.org/10.1037/ccp0000636.

8. Ciao et al., "Inclusive Dissonance-Based Body Image Interventions."

9. Nicole Byer, "Nicole Byer on How to Love Yourself" (interview with Sam Sander), *It's Been a Minute* (podcast), NPR, June 30, 2020, https://www.npr.org/2020/06/24/883053349/nicole-byer-on-how-to-love-yourself.

10. Byer interview with Sam Sander, https://www.npr.org/2020/06/24/883053349/nicole-byer-on-how-to-love-yourself.

11. Giles Hattersley, "Adele, Reborn: The British Icon Gets Candid About Divorce, Body Image, Romance & Her 'Self-Redemption' Record," *British Vogue*, October 7, 2021, https://www.vogue.co.uk/arts-and-lifestyle/article/adele-british-vogue-interview.

12. Claudia Rankine, "Lizzo on Hope, Justice, and the Election," *Vogue*, September 24, 2020, https://www.vogue.com/article/lizzo-cover-october-2020.

CHAPTER 6: CAN WE EAT OUR WAY TO LIBERATION?

1. Edmund Lee, "The White Issue: Has Anna Wintour's Diversity Push Come Too Late?" *New York Times*, published October 24, 2020, updated December 15, 2020, https://www.nytimes.com/2020/10/24/business/media/anna-wintour-vogue-race.html.

2. Tamar Adler, "All You Can Eat? Inside the Intuitive Eating Craze," *Vogue*, February 14, 2020, https://www.vogue.com/article/inside-the -intuitive-eating-craze.

3. Lee, "The White Issue."

4. Evelyn Tribole and Elyse Resch, *Intuitive Eating*, 4th ed. (New York: St. Martin's Essentials, 2020).

5. "Food Security and Nutrition Assistance," USDA Economic Research Service, updated July 19, 2022, https://www.ers.usda.gov/data-products /ag-and-food-statistics-charting-the-essentials/food-security-and-nutrition -assistance/#:~:text=The%20prevalence%20of%20food%20insecurity,had %20very%20low%20food%20security.

6. Carol Pogash, "Free Lunch Isn't Cool, So Some Students Go Hungry," *New York Times*, March 1, 2008, https://www.nytimes.com/2008/03/01 /education/01lunch.html.

7. Colleen Christensen, no.food.rules, on Instagram at https://www .instagram.com/no.food.rules.

CHAPTER 7: HEALTH IS KILLING US

1. Katherine M. Flegal, "The Obesity Wars and the Education of a Researcher: A Personal Account," *Progress in Cardiovascular Diseases* 67 (July–August 2021): 75–79, https://doi.org/10.1016/j.pcad.2021.06.009.

2. Virginia Hughes, "The Big Fat Truth," *Nature* 497 (2013): 428–430, https://doi.org/10.1038/497428a.

3. Charles B. Davenport, "Research in Eugenics," *Science* 54, no. 1400 (October 28, 1921): 391–397, https://doi.org/10.1126/science.54.1400.391.

4. J. H. Kellogg, "Relation of Public Health to Race Degeneracy," *American Journal of Public Health* 4, no. 8 (August 1, 1914): 649–663, https://doi .org/10.2105/AJPH.4.8.649.

5. Flegal, "The Obesity Wars," 75–79.

6. Robert Crawford, "Healthism and the Medicalization of Everyday Life," *International Journal of Health Services* 10, no. 3 (1980), https://doi .org/10.2190/3H2H-3XJN-3KAY-G9NY.

7. Harriet A. Washington, *Medical Apartheid: The Dark History of Medical Experimentation on Black Americans from Colonial Times to the Present* (New York: Doubleday, 2006), 19–20.

8. Alison Conrad, Jen Zuckerman, Gizem Templeton, and Project Team, "Identifying and Countering White Supremacy Culture in Food Systems," World Food Policy Center, Duke Sanford, https://wfpc.sanford.duke.edu /research/identifying-and-countering-white-supremacy-culture-in-food -systems/.

9. Nina Sevilla, "Food Apartheid: Racialized Access to Healthy Affordable Food," NRDC, April 2, 2021, https://www.nrdc.org/experts/nina-sevilla /food-apartheid-racialized-access-healthy-affordable-food.

10. Conrad et al., "Identifying and Countering White Supremacy Culture in Food Systems."

11. Robert A. Ersek, Henry Newton Bell IV, and Aurelio Vazquez Salisbury, "Serial and Superficial Suction for Steatopygia (Hottentot Bustle)," *Aesthetic Plastic Surgery* 18, no. 3 (1994): 279–282, https://www.doi.org /10.1007/BF00449795; Justin Parkinson, "The Significance of Sarah Baartman," *BBC News Magazine*, January 7, 2016, https://www.bbc.com/news /magazine-35240987.

12. Washington, *Medical Apartheid*, 36.

13. Da'Shaun L. Harrison, *Belly of the Beast: The Politics of Anti-Fatness as Anti-Blackness* (Berkeley: North Atlantic Books, 2021), 35.

14. Trevor Butterworth, "Top Science Journal Rebukes Harvard's Top Nutritionist," *Forbes*, May 27, 2013, https://www.forbes.com/sites /trevorbutterworth/2013/05/27/top-science-journal-rebukes-harvards-top-nutritionist/?sh=693158b8173b.

CHAPTER 8: GOOPED, BUT NOT WELL

1. Home page, Goop, https://goop.com.

2. "Moon Dust," Moon Juice, https://moonjuice.com/collections/dust.

3. Home page, Hydration Room, https://www.hydrationroom.com.

4. Noam Scheiber, "Tesla Employee's Firing and Elon Musk Tweet on Union Were Illegal, Labor Board Rules," *New York Times*, published

March 25, 2021, updated May 7, 2021, https://www.nytimes.com/2021/03/25/business/musk-labor-board.html.

5. About page, Poosh, https://poosh.com/about/.

6. "What Is Non-Western Medicine?" Shakthi Health & Wellness Center, https://www.raowellness.com/what-is-non-western-medicine/.

7. "Overview," Healthy Kitchens Healthy Lives, https://www.healthykitchens.org/overview.

8. David Eisenberg, slide 1 in "The State of Nutrition Science Before, During, and After the COVID-19 Pandemic" (presentation at Healthy Kitchens, Healthy Lives, Napa Valley, CA, February 2, 2022).

9. Alvin Powell, "Patterns of Obesity Prove Resilient," *Harvard Gazette*, November 25, 2015, https://news.harvard.edu/gazette/story/2015/11/patterns-of-obesity-prove-resilient.

CHAPTER 9: REWRITING THE NARRATIVE

1. "Mission and Vision," Sins Invalid, https://www.sinsinvalid.org/mission.

2. Brené Brown, "The Power of Vulnerability," TED Talk, 20:03, December 2010, https://www.ted.com/talks/brene_brown_the_power_of_vulnerability.

3. Brown, "The Power of Vulnerability."

4. About page, Brené Brown, https://brenebrown.com/about.

5. Brown, "The Power of Vulnerability."

Index